PERSONAL
ETHICS

PERSONAL ETHICS

By

B. H. STREETER, K. E. KIRK
J. P. R. MAUD, C. R. MORRIS
R. L. HALL, R. C. MORTIMER
J. S. BEZZANT

Edited by

KENNETH E. KIRK

REGIUS PROFESSOR OF MORAL AND
PASTORAL THEOLOGY, AND CANON
OF CHRIST CHURCH, OXFORD

Essay Index Reprint Series

BOOKS FOR LIBRARIES PRESS

FREEPORT, NEW YORK

First published 1934
Reprinted 1968

LIBRARY OF CONGRESS CATALOG CARD NUMBER:
68-22921

PRINTED IN THE UNITED STATES OF AMERICA

CONTENTS

INTRODUCTION

THE following lectures are published much in the form in which they were delivered (by the kind permission of the Provost and Fellows) in Queen's College Hall, in the Michaelmas Term of 1933. There was no previous consultation between the lecturers as to the method of treatment to be adopted, nor yet as to the results to be arrived at. Each followed his own bent, and no one of them is responsible either for the arguments or for the conclusions of any of the others. Nor, in so far as any lecturer might be assumed to apply already formed principles to his subject, was it in any way taken for granted that those principles would be the same for all. It is fair to every one concerned to state these facts as clearly as possible, but their recognition adds interest to the book. For it will not escape the reader's attention that the method of approach is very much the same in each lecture; and that identical principles tend to reappear in slightly varied form throughout the book.

This similarity, no doubt, is due in part to the actual willingness of the lecturers to co-operate in a single series under the general title of 'Personal Ethics'. But it is perhaps not irrelevant to suggest that the agreement goes deeper than might have been expected from this circumstance alone. Nor does it seem to be beyond the legitimate scope of an editorial introduction to point out four principal characteristics which the lectures have in common, and to suggest that they present in miniature a conspectus of the position which ethical inquiry has now established for itself amid the fluctuations and uncertainties of post-war thought.

(*a*) There is a general agreement that the problems of practical ethics demand a treatment at once more respectful and less cavalier than is meted out by those who say 'It's only the motive that matters'; or (alternatively) 'It is impossible to generalize; everything depends upon the circumstances of the particular case'. As regards the first of these two methods of burking inquiry, no one, of course, is going to be so foolish as to deny that motives *do* matter, and matter intensely. But quite distinct from any conviction we have on the question of motives is the conviction that we can—and indeed *must*—discuss the question of 'duties', or obligations, as incurred by us in virtue of the situations in which from time to time we find ourselves placed, without reference to the motives from which we shall perform those duties if we do indeed perform them. The world of serious thought, in fact, is once more asking for an objective treatment of the problem of duty; and it is becoming more natural than it has been for some time past for writers on ethics to attempt to comply with the demand.

In respect of the second aphorism, again, no one will be concerned to deny that an immediate duty in one specific set of circumstances will not necessarily be a duty at all in an entirely different set of circumstances.

But this does not mean, as the aphorism suggests, that generalization is impossible and discussion (in consequence) futile. It still remains possible to generalize as to the *sorts* of circumstances which tend to impose particular duties upon us. Each set of circumstances has indeed a uniqueness of its own, just as any individual animal or tree has; but in neither case is it a uniqueness which sets it in an exclusive 'kind' by itself, and exempts it from the operation of all the laws or principles which apply to other 'kinds'. There is of course always the possibility that when we find ourselves in a particular set of circumstances we shall discover some factor which removes it from the 'kind' to which we should antecedently have expected it to belong. But this does not mean that it now forms a 'kind' of which it is the only representative, and which is thus incapable of being generalized, but merely that it has been transferred to another 'kind' to which general principles apply as before.

(*b*) Again, the lecturers appear to agree that an exact understanding of circumstances is necessary before duties can be determined. The 'personal ethics' of the modern Englishman, for example, must reckon with the fact that the English educational system is dichotomized by the line which separates the 'Public Schools' from the other types of secondary school; they must reckon with the predominance and stability of the 'middle classes' in English society : and with the fact that industry and distribution in modern England are still organized on a capitalist basis. We may perhaps wish that any or all of these things were not so; we may even be working for a revolution which shall put an end to them. But in the meantime we have to live with things and people as they are; and it is idle to say that we have no other duties than to hasten on the revolution—such a statement is meaningless when we have to decide how much to spend on a summer holiday, or where to have our children educated. Our duties are duties which oblige in the present state of society; for it is in that state that we have to live and act.

But although our personal ethics are to be the ethics of to-day and not of to-morrow, they must also avoid being a mere *réchauffé* of the ethics of yesterday. No doubt there are principles which are eternal and not transitory; each of the contributors to this book would probably agree that what he was attempting to do was to adapt the universal ideal of 'Christian citizenship' to the particular problem discussed by him as it appears under contemporary conditions. But the point is that the principle *has* to be so adapted if it is to be of any practical value; vague generalizations and flamboyant rhetoric will not advance the cause of sober attention to the call of duty.

(*c*) It will be noticed, further, that what the lecturers mean by 'personal' ethics includes much which in earlier days might well have been called 'public' or 'social' ethics. This implies that for the world of to-day the scope of personal responsibility has been enlarged to an almost unlimited extent. We shall all

agree to regard this as a proper and welcome development in our ideas about conduct; and in any case
it is probably inevitable wherever the general conditions of thought deserve to be called democratic—
wherever, that is to say, they urge the individual to
look on life with the eyes of a statesman, as though he
might at any moment be called upon to direct the
destinies of society. 'If I were King' is perhaps at
best no more than the expression of a simple desire
for power to redress wrongs from which the subject
himself has suffered; but 'If I were Prime Minister'
or 'President of the Board of Education' is a challenge
to serious and responsible thought. So education,
economics, nationalism, and the like become problems about which it is the individual's duty to think
impartially; and as to which (so long as we enjoy our
present relative freedom of speech, thought, and
action in respect of these and similar matters) he has
the possibility, and in consequence the duty, of influ-
encing the trend of events however slightly in the
direction of that state of things which he believes
ought to be realized.

(*d*) Thus although the ethics of to-day must be
the ethics of to-day and not of to-morrow, this is
not to say that they are not largely *concerned* with
to-morrow. 'My duty to posterity' has always been
an accepted category of ethics; but our modern biological methods of thought, with their insistence upon
the importance of the race (often, it may be, even at
the expense of the individual), have given it excep-

tional prominence in contemporary theory. To work for a revolution (which may be none the less a revolution for being gradual and peaceful) whose fruits will not be gathered in the present generation, or perhaps for many generations to come, is no longer an optional counsel of perfection; it has been adopted into the fibre of every serious man's scheme of duties. For obvious reasons, this principle is less prominent in some of the lectures which follow than in others, but it is probably true to say that it is present to the minds of all the contributors alike.

It is common knowledge that the philosophic thought of to-day is more actively concerned with the theory of ethics than it has been for some considerable time. The course of lectures here brought together and presented to the reader was devised as a symbol of a similar activity of thought about practical ethical problems. That such an activity is widespread cannot be denied. I do not suppose that those who have collaborated in this book would wish their lectures to be regarded as anything more than tentative contributions towards the discussion of problems whose difficulties are patent to all. They would indeed claim that the main positions, which they have individually adopted in respect of their particular subjects, are the result of serious consideration, but they would not profess to have followed out the corollaries of what they have written to the extent which would be necessitated by a formal treatise. Least of all would they wish it to be thought that they had written in any dogmatic or doctrinaire spirit. They are inquirers, as are all other men of goodwill: and the present book is no more than a presentation of the first results of their inquiries.

K. E. K.

I. EDUCATION

By B. H. STREETER

THE relation of Education to Ethics was a question much debated in the ancient Greek world. Plato's *Republic*—a work whose artistry beguiles even those who have to 'get it up' for examination purposes—is to a large degree a treatise on this subject. And it is sufficiently obvious that the production of such a work implies the existence of a public already interested in the problem and trained by much previous debate to appreciate its issues.

During the Middle Ages the debate ceased. Education, such as there was, was carried on in the monastery. Naturally it was assumed that Theology was Queen of the Sciences, and that the ethical values implied in the theology, and produced by the discipline, of the Church admitted of discussion only in points of detail. With the Renaissance discussion reawoke.

The Renaissance was an ethical, even more than an intellectual, revolt from the Middle Ages; but since its inspiration was the 'New Learning', and its weapon the new education, it seemed on the continent of Europe to be primarily intellectual and aesthetic. But ethically it was a revolution in that it was a dethronement of the 'other-worldliness' of the medieval outlook, and a reaffirmation of the value of knowledge and art for their own sake. With this went a reassertion of the claims of the individual and of the right to, and value of, an all-round self-development. The French Revolution was a further assertion of the freedom of the individual and his right to self-development, especially in the political and social sphere; and to the spread of the spirit of the Revolution over Europe the career of Bismarck was the first serious check. In France itself—as more recently in Russia—the revolt was quite as much against the Church and its traditions as against monarchy and aristocratic rule.

Thus it came to be more and more taken for granted on the continent of Europe that education (at any rate, what we call the Higher Education) is primarily concerned with things intellectual and aesthetic; and that its main function is the development of the individual and his capacities. In England, however, this conception of education has never been dominant. It is often forgotten that educational development in England, quite as much as political development, has shown in essentials a marked contrast to that of the continent of Europe. The English public school, and the college system at Oxford and Cambridge, differ from the corresponding stages of education on the Continent as much as do the British monarchy and parliamentary system from their counterparts elsewhere in Europe. Indeed they differ more; for political evolution on the Continent has often resulted from conscious attempts on a national scale to imitate the British constitution; but imitation of English education has been attempted only sporadically and by occasional individuals.

The difference between England and the Continent in educational aim and method may be attributed to four main causes :

(1) The Renaissance and the Reformation came to England at *the same time*, and as incidents in what may be called the period of national adolescence. You cannot separate the streams of influence represented by the names of Raleigh and Drake, Shakespeare and Bacon, Cranmer, Colet, and the translators of the Bible. Every one of these is characteristically English; and they were all, so to speak, rowing in the same boat. On the Continent, however, the Reformation, so far from being an aspect of the Renaissance, was largely a reaction against it; and the lines of division which it produced cut right across those of nationality.

(2) The political development of England from the time of Elizabeth has centred round the vindication of individual liberty on its political side. Political liberty was steadily achieved; but only as a result of a struggle sufficiently severe to preoccupy the national attention for centuries. What the Englishman fought for and achieved was free speech and freedom of the person; he was not specially interested in an educational development which mainly stimulated free thought. In France it was otherwise. Among a vigorous people, liberty suppressed in one direction will break out in another; the counterpart of the political

system impersonated in Louis XIV was the cultural tradition which produced Voltaire.

(3) The principle *cuius regio eius religio* sounded obvious to the continental mind; its application could hardly be rigorous in an island where it would mean that the King must change his religion whenever he crossed the River Tweed. The fact that Scotland was Presbyterian, combined with the tolerance and dislike of cruelty native to the English temper, caused the penalty of nonconformity to be, not persecution of the continental type, but merely political disabilities. Persecution, if sufficiently rigorous and persistent, may obliterate a religious minority; disabilities are more likely to stimulate and strengthen it. But a minority subject to political disabilities inevitably welcomes political change. Thus in England the mere existence of nonconformity meant, more especially during the nineteenth century, that one of the most vigorous strains in the national religion was on the side of change, political and social. Christianity was associated with the fight for democracy as well as with resistance to it. In sharp contrast to this has been the position of religion in the national life of Austria and France, and in the Protestant states of Germany, where 'nonconformity' has been a politically negligible factor. That is why on the Continent religion in the popular mind is more or less identified with the support of the political *status quo*. There are grounds for the taunt that it is 'the opiate of the people'.

(4) It has been pointed out that the four greater streams into which Western Christianity divided in the sixteenth century continue the influence, and reproduce the spirit, of four notable personalities. Ignatius Loyola, the founder of the Jesuit Order, recreated the Roman Church of the Counter-Reformation. Luther impressed the type of mysticism, implied in his interpretation of the doctrine of Justification by Faith, on much of Germany and Scandinavia. Calvin gave to Protestantism a temper more crusading—international, practical, and democratic. Calvinism influenced England, inside as well as outside the National Church; nevertheless the influence and the name which best typifies the spirit of the Church of England is that of Erasmus. Erasmus stood for what Matthew Arnold was later on to speak of as the fusion of Hebraism and Hellenism—the Hebraic element being predominantly the stress on conduct. Nonconformity also, here following the lead of Calvin, agreed with Anglicanism in stressing the ethical element in religion; whereas Romanism and Lutheranism alike, though in very different ways, give greater weight to its mystical side.

The result of this religious heritage on the English conception of education during the last hundred years cannot be overstated. The Hellenic or 'latitudinarian' strain in the Anglican tradition made it both possible and natural for educational reformers like Arnold and Jowett to see in such reform a most practical expression of religion. And, from the ethical stress in English religion, it has followed that, whereas on the Continent it has been assumed that education is primarily concerned with the intellectual and aesthetic development of the individual, it has equally been taken for granted in England that character is its most essential element. The reform of the public school system initiated by Thomas Arnold asserted this in the sphere of upper and middle-class education. Its acceptance in that of popular education is evidenced by the fact that elementary education in England has so largely been carried on by religious bodies assisted by state funds. When secular schools were started, there was unanimous insistence that religion should be an element in the school curriculum —an insistence strong enough to survive the endless difficulties created by the wrangles of the Churches about the precise type of that religious instruction. A national conviction that character training is essential to sound education is the background against which the historian must study the long political struggles as to whether the Bible alone or the Bible plus the Church Catechism should be taught in the schools of the country. Only in a country where it was taken for granted that education is necessarily concerned with ethics would the public have tolerated so long the interminable quarrels as to the precise denominational flavour to be given along with the ethics.

But the educational methods and ideals which flourished respectively in England and on the Continent at the end of the nineteenth century are at the present moment challenged by two new potentialities. First, the disposition of the modern State to use education as a purely political instrument and its increasing power of doing so. Secondly, the possible exploitation of the results of the branch of study known as the New Psychology.

The Power of the State. The first large-scale attempts in modern times to use education as a political instrument were made by Germany and by Japan. Bismarck visualized the political problem of the New German Empire as primarily twofold. First, there was the problem of cementing into a single nation a number of communities which for many centuries had been independent sovereign states, often at war with one another. Secondly, there was the problem of so organizing and directing the strength of this newly founded Empire that it might become, and remain permanently, the predominant military power in Europe. The system of education developed in Germany in the state schools—and practically all schools there were state schools—was one which quite consciously, and extremely effectively, tended to create the spirit of militarist nationalism. It fostered the virtues as well as the defects which go with that ideal. Its emotional focus was the inculcation of loyalty to an Imperial House—crowned with the halo of romance as successor to the glorious memories of Charlemagne. Not till the outbreak of the Great War was it recognized outside Germany how largely this system had been successful in changing the temper of the people, or rather in diffusing over the whole Reich the typical virtues and defects of the Prussian character.

A country which, at about the same period, found itself faced with a problem to some extent analogous was Japan. In the national sense Japan had no need to unify herself; but she had realized that national independence could not be saved unless within a short period of years she could revolutionize her traditional culture by appropriating the knowledge and inventions of the West. To that end, quite definitely and with extreme thoroughness, her educational system was planned. This system resembled the German in the emphasis laid on loyalty to the throne. The incredibly difficult task of passing from an immemorial native culture to one evolved by remote and alien races demanded an emotionally potent and augustly romantic motive power. The moral and emotional focus of the change was found in the restoration of political power to a House immemorially sacred. National independence was threatened on the mainland by the military power of Russia and at sea by the naval powers of the Pacific. Thus in Japan as in Germany the educational system was purposely designed to extend and adapt to modern uses the fighting spirit of the Samurai caste, while diverting to the person of the Emperor the Samurai's devotion to his feudal lord.

But of late years there has come into view a new and more sinister phase in the exploitation of educational possibilities for political ends. This is the result of the discovery made during the War of the political value of 'propaganda'. It has been found that people's opinions and actions can be directed by agencies of a quasi-educational character long after school years. Unlimited possibilities of this seem to be afforded by state control of the press, the wireless, and the cinema. This has led to a development in certain countries of what is really a form of adult education directed to definite political ends. By this I mean, not so much political ends in detail, as the creation in a people of that type of national ideal and national ethic which seems to the rulers for the time being to be politically desirable.

The most thorough-going experiment of this kind is being tried in Russia. Here not only what ordinarily goes under the name of education, but the whole of the intellectual, literary, and aesthetic activities of the nation is entirely determined by the political creed of the ruling party; and the moral ideals inculcated are precisely and exclusively those which this party approves.

Methods and aims essentially of the same kind are being elaborated by Fascism in Italy and by the German Nazis. Both of these make a great parade of their hostility to Communism; but they fight it with its own weapons. If anything, they go farther than Communism in their frantic denial of the value of liberty, and in their assertion of the right of a ruling faction to regiment news and opinion.

The avowed object of these state-controlled systems is to make a whole people so far as possible to think alike on all political and moral subjects. National docility would seem to be a prerequisite condition for the initial success of such a policy; and apparently enough of this exists in Italy where the Church, in Germany and Russia where Church and State alike, have for centuries made obedience the primary virtue. It may turn out to be fortunate for humanity that docility is a quality which the national traditions of England, France, and America have never tended to exalt.

There is one point which specially concerns ourselves in Oxford to note. Pre-war experiments in producing or modifying national ethics and ideals by means of education were in the main confined to the schools; Communism, Fascism, and the Nazi movement avowedly and without disguise extend this system to the universities. From the standpoint of the educationalist this fact is one of the most formidable as well as the most deplorable in the modern world. Whatever else may be the merits of propaganda, it is not the expression of a disinterested love of truth. But education at the university level is a mockery unless it is inspired by the worship of truth. At the university level knowledge ceases to be knowledge unless it is the expression of the spirit of research. And, except in the sphere of physical science, research is impossible without liberty of opinion.

Turn now to the ancient world. The ideal of education which was in general prevalent on the continent of Europe from the Renaissance to the end of the nineteenth century was more or less consciously a revival under modern conditions of the spirit of the great age of Athens. It was an education which encouraged the utmost freedom of thought and the development of the intellectual and aesthetic capacity of the individual. On the other hand the ancient counterpart of Communist and Fascist education is to be found in Sparta—the extreme instance in antiquity of a lifelong education of the citizen to be merely an obedient unit in the state machine. It we try to read the lesson of history, we cannot but reflect that, with all its faults and failures, Athenian liberty left to the world a richer inheritance than has been left by any other state of the same size or in so short a time. What has Sparta left behind? Strong but fruitless, heroic but barren; her virtues availed to bring about the fall of Athens. The analogy is one which gives us pause.

But we cannot understand or explain movements like Communism or Fascism, unless we recognize in them the moral basis, from which arises their strength and their wide measure of support by public opinion in the countries which they dominate. Their power is not merely due to political or economic contingencies, external and internal; it largely results from the fact that for a century or more in these countries the emphasis in education has been mainly on aesthetic and intellectual development—individualistic and self-centred. Against this kind of individualism Fascism, Nazism, and Communism are ethical and spiritual reactions. In the countries where they prevail the obscurantism—either political or intellectual or both—of the Churches had long ago produced a revolt from Christianity on the part alike of the intelligenzia and the artisan. Deprived of the moral inspiration of the old religion, yet dissatisfied with the alternative of a self-centred individualism, these have long been seeking for a dynamic ideal to save them from personal and national demoralization. Fascism and Communism have power, because they present such an ideal, and present it practically *as a religion*. 'God is dead'; but Italy is on the march. Religion is the opiate of the slave; but man is throwing off his chains.

I do not belittle the extent to which these movements are the result of economic conditions, and of the political consequences of the Great War. But considered as ideals—and it is as ideals that they have driving power—they are largely a reaction against a too exclusively Athenian tradition in educational emphasis, along with the association of Christianity either with intellectually impossible beliefs or with political conservatism. But that means that they are a reaction against something different from what has prevailed in this country. Just for that reason it is likely to be the more difficult for either Communism or Fascism to take England by storm; and therefore we may hope that in English education the great tradition of free thought and free speech may still continue. The Communist, the Fascist, and the Nazi have rediscovered the fact that intellectual cultivation apart from character development produces persons who are a burden to themselves and a disease to the community. In England that fact, most fortunately, does not require to be rediscovered; it has never been forgotten. The English school tradition has emphasized just that conception of personal loyalty and of the duty of the individual to the community which are being re-emphasized by foreign movements to-day. Their re-emphasis is an over-emphasis, to the point of distortion. For emphasis on *esprit de corps* and public service will produce a Spartan sterility unless it is on the basis of, and is accompanied by, an equally vigorous assertion of individual liberty and of the duty and virtue of self-reliance.

But the English tradition has had two grave defects. First, the public school system was evolved to deal with the training of a limited class, a class which was in the past the ruling class in this country. Secondly, it neither aimed at, nor succeeded in developing on the intellectual side those characteristics of initiative and adventure which it had developed on the practical side. The first aim, then, of the educationalist in this country should be to do for the intellectual side of public school education what Thomas Arnold did for the moral and practical. The second aim should be, so far as possible, to make the common property of the nation an educational tradition, moral and intellectual, which must first be developed in the public schools. Such a tradition necessarily, for economic and other reasons, must *originate* in a limited class; but once created it can be indefinitely extended. Japan succeeded in making the virtues of the old Samurai caste the common property of the nation. Why should not England do the same for those of a reformed and widened public school system?

The New Psychology. Next to the enhanced power and changing disposition of the state, the potentialities of the New Psychology claim the attention of the modern educationalist. I can merely call attention to the existence of one of the problems raised by this study; and space does not permit me properly to develop even this.

Homo animal rationale. No formula has come down to us with greater authority and iteration in academic tradition. True, the statement *Man is a rational animal* is one which facts do not always seem to bear out; but in past ages to point this out was to brand oneself a cynic. Nowadays, under the influence of the New Psychology, fashion demands that we affirm precisely the opposite—to an extent which almost eliminates the claims of man to possess any rationality at all.

Darwin taught us that biologically man is one of the higher mammals. Psychologists insist that this generalization covers not only his physical structure, but also his apparatus of inherited instincts. But between man and other mammals there is one great difference: in the lower animals instinct is adjusted to environment so well that, if as occasion arises the animal acts in the way which instinct prompts, such action is usually that best adapted to the welfare of the individual and still more of the species. A similar state of things no doubt existed with the animal ancestors of man, perhaps even with his subhuman ancestors. But at a very early stage man began to complicate his environment by using tools, by building houses, by sowing fields and otherwise planning for a distant future—thus necessarily accumulating property and organizing society, and so forth. Every further advance towards civilization means that the environment to which man must adjust himself becomes more and more complicated. His environment, therefore, becomes continually more unlike the environment with which his remote ancestors could cope by an almost automatic reaction to stimulus in accordance with the immediate dictates of instinct. Thus every fresh advance in civilization widens the chasm between merely instinctive response to environment and the kind of action which is best for the individual and for the species.

This maladjustment of the instinctual organization of man to the demands of the artificial environment into which in civilized countries he is born, explains— or at any rate partially explains—the phenomenon known to our ancestors as Original Sin. The human race is in an unfortunate predicament. It has created civilization in order to live better; but the higher the civilization the greater the difficulty of living in it at all, or, at any rate, at all well.

The primary task, then, of the educationalist (in so far as he is concerned with the training of character) is to assist the child and the adolescent to solve for themselves this problem of original maladjustment. The New Psychology is equally averse to the Augustinian doctrine of Original Sin and to the theory of the 'noble savage', which was the eighteenth-century reaction against that doctrine. It would seem, then, equally to condemn educational methods based on either of those views. A method which, having wrongly diagnosed the disease as Original Sin, proceeds to treat it accordingly, will necessarily lead to bad results. But neither will you get the best results from an education based on the theory of an original perfection of human nature; for that in effect denies that there is any maladjustment to be overcome. On the Augustinian diagnosis it logically follows that the problem of moral education is primarily one of inhibition and the suppression of evil instincts. In medieval Oxford there was a degree of Master of Grammar which qualified for the post of teacher in schools controlled by the University. Office in the Middle Ages was normally conferred by transferring to its holder the instrument which best symbolized its essential nature—as the Crown to the King, the Keys to the Chancellor. On this principle, when the degree of Master of Grammar was conferred, the recipient was handed a rod; and he 'incepted' (i.e. entered upon the rights of the degree) by flogging a boy 'openlye in the Scolys'.[1] This conception of the essentials of educational method survived till Victorian days; witness the story of the mother who said to the governess, 'Go and see what Mary and Billy are doing; and tell them they mustn't'.

Educational reform during the last forty years has been largely a reaction against this tradition. Some theorists have gone to the extent of eliminating from education the element of discipline. But such theories under-estimate the magnitude of the maladjustment to be overcome by the normal child and adolescent; they fail to measure the width of the chasm which cannot but exist between instinctive animal reaction and moral behaviour in civilized society. Moral personality is not given to man ready-made. Indeed the real nature of the problem becomes clear only if we ask why any solution at all is possible. Why is it that the human animal can be so trained that he becomes a possible member of a civilized society? Why are we not all criminals?

The answer to this question lies in the single fact that of all animals man is *the most teachable*. Most of the lower animals have some capacity for learning; that is, they can be trained to a limited extent to react to stimuli in a way other than that prompted by native

[1] H. Rashdall, *Universities in the Middle Ages*, vol. ii, pt. ii, p. 599.

instinct. Some animals are much more teachable than
others; a sheep-dog can be taught to carry out quite
complicated orders, a monkey to perform elaborate
tricks, and fame has been won by a 'learned pig'. But
man is immeasurably more teachable than any of
these; at any rate, some men are. This capacity for
learning is generally explained by saying that he has
greater intelligence. That is part of the explanation,
perhaps the larger part; but a part of the explanation
only a little less important is the enhanced power possessed by man of holding up the natural and immediate
instinctive reaction to stimulus, while he reflects in
which of several possible ways he will react to it, or
whether he will inhibit action altogether. To take a
commonplace example: I am sitting in a bus and a
heavy man staggers in and treads upon my corn. To
this particular stimulus the instinctive animal reaction
is to stand up and hit the man on the jaw. But I have
the power of inhibiting that instinctive reaction, while
I reflect whether he did it on purpose, or perhaps
because he was drunk, or merely because the bus
lurched; and having so reflected I shall probably be
led—if not from motives of humanity, at least of prudence—to react to the stimulus in some other way; or
possibly even to inhibit speech and action altogether.

I stress this obvious point because popular literature has made a great deal of play with a misunderstanding of the true meaning of the technical term
'repression' as it is used by psychologists. It is frequently supposed that psychology discountenances the

use of that capacity for inhibiting instinctive reactions which we commonly speak of as 'self-control'. Life in a society is possible only if the members of it have some self-control. More than this, self-control is a primary condition of the development of a unified and coherent personality; without it the individual is an emotional weathercock. Even a criminal must have some self-control, or he would never have acquired sufficient capacity for reasoned action to enable him to commit a crime.

'Repression', in the technical sense in which the word is used by psychologists, is a name given to experiences which present two essential features: (i) they happen in early life—mostly before the age of seven; (ii) they are themselves forgotten, but, like an unhealthy tooth, they have become a source of a kind of poisoning of the system. 'Repression' in the technical psychological sense is an entirely different thing from self-control, that capacity of pulling oneself up to think before one acts, which is the first condition of the development of a stable personality.

But though psychology does not condemn that conscious inhibition of instinctive reactions which is a necessary part of self-control, it has taught us that it is not psychologically sound to base an ethic on the inculcation of a purely negative self-control. Social life, even at the savage level, is impossible without some inhibition of instinctive response to stimulus; but that educational system is most successful which seeks to provide what is technically known as a 'sublimation' of the inhibited instinct. If the steam in a boiler has reached a certain amount of pressure before the time to start the engine, it finds its way out through the safety valve. Similarly, it is the business of the educationalist and of the sociologist to invent safety valves by means of which an instinct, when denied its animal expression, can find an alternative employment.

Human personality, however, being a more complicated thing than a steam boiler, needs something more than a mere safety valve. In a well-run school or a well-ordered society the spare energy—which at the animal level would exhaust itself in reproduction of the species, acquiring food or fighting enemies— will be re-directed, or 'sublimated', towards ends which are not merely harmless, but are also valuable for the life of the community and for the further development of the personality of the individual. Superfluous sex instinct may be sublimated into aesthetic interests; superfluous combativeness may be expressed in games, which are beneficial for the physical and moral development of the individual, or may be directed towards competitive excellence in activities of a useful and constructive character; and so on and so forth.

Here again we find a notable difference between the English and the continental practice, both in education and in the national conception of the nature and function of law. On the Continent, especially in the Roman Catholic and Lutheran tradition, the primary virtue has always been *obedience*. In England, on the other hand, stress has been rather on the idea of the *responsibility* which goes with the possession of freedom. This was especially emphasized in the public school ideal initiated by Arnold, where the moral motive in the last resort boils down to *noblesse oblige*. Even obedience is subsumed under this motive, for reasonable obedience to a properly constituted authority is a thing which 'a decent person' will freely accord.

The same thing is true of the English approach to the conception of law. I remember a German student who was in Oxford before the War telling me of his surprise at the action of a policeman who stopped him riding a bicycle without a light after dusk. The policeman merely said to him, 'Look here, Sir, you ought not to be doing this, you might run into some one. Just light up.' A German policeman would have felt that the law had been broken and must be vindicated. That is to say, whereas the English policeman thought of the law as a reasonable rule which a reasonable person, once it was pointed out to him, would obey, the German thought of it as an ideal principle whose majesty must be vindicated by punishment.

In recent years *self-expression* has been a catchword which, for many, has almost acquired the odour of sanctity—in matters of art as well as in matters of ethics. In the doctrine of self-expression in the sphere of art, the Chinese had anticipated the West by eight hundred years. But they had the good sense to draw the corollary that, if an essential element is self-expression, then the value of a work of art must depend on the quality of the self of which it is the expression. In other words, self-expression is valuable, or the contrary, according to the quality of the personality to be expressed. That the same thing holds in the case of ethics is a proposition that would seem to need no arguing.

From the purely psychological point of view, the only type of self of which the expression is likely to be valuable is a self so developed that it has (so far as is possible) reached the point of overcoming the original maladjustment between instinct and environment, which is the original problem of character training. Life is conflict, and till life ends, conflict *external* to the self will necessarily continue. But internal conflict is a thing which can be—at any rate approximately—resolved into a harmony; and the achievement of this internal harmony is the greatest asset of the individual in the external conflicts with which he will necessarily be faced.

Now an ethic based on law, conceived of as something externally enforced, is necessarily an ethic of inhibition, and, therefore, is one which must from its own nature provoke internal conflict, even though it results in a course of conduct which externally may seem stable and sane. Though of course the intensity of the internal conflict will vary with the extent to which the law is recognized as valuable; and it will also vary enormously with the vitality of the individual and with details in his psychological history.

It is in the light of this difference between the English and the continental mind that I understand the contention of Freud that morality is essentially a set of rules forced by society upon the unwilling individual. This conception might hold of children brought up in some English homes; but not in the majority, where good conduct is normally inculcated as something which is reasonable or kind, and the moral motive is 'Decent people behave so and so', that is, *noblesse oblige*. Freud is by birth a Jew who inherits the conception of religion as primarily law; he practises in a country where ethical tradition has been formed by the legalistic authoritarianism of the Roman Church and the political heritage of an autocratic government. The point then, which I wish to make, is that Freud's conception is exactly that of another famous Jew—I mean St. Paul, before he became a Christian. From the Epistles to the Romans and Galatians it is evident that to St. Paul the word 'law' implies a system of ethic, imposed from without upon a recalcitrant individual, albeit recognized by him as majestic in its claim to obedience. That was why, when he became a Christian, the change seemed to him to be primarily one of *liberation*—liberation from the dominance of that kind of external rule which the individual, though bound to reverence it, cannot but, in his inmost being, resent.

To St. Paul the Gospel was 'good news' precisely

because it meant liberation from an ethic based upon inhibitions. For the reiterated 'Thou shalt not' of the Ten Commandments, there is substituted, 'Thou shalt love thy neighbour as thyself'; but for him this was not merely the substitution of the positive precept 'do good' for the negative 'don't do harm'; it was also an ethic of self-expression. And it was this because the new self which now found its natural expression in loving its neighbour was no longer, like the old self, a bird in a cage, cribbed, cabined, and confined by inhibitory law; it was a self transformed and re-created by the inward appropriation of a new conception of God and a new relation of the self to God which made all men potentially 'sons of God'. Thus 'Love God and love thy neighbour as thyself' become no longer precepts of obedience, but the means of spontaneous self-expression.

II. MARRIAGE

By K. E. KIRK

THE problem of marriage is a sub-division of the problem of sex. We may define it as the search for the best method of regulating the ordinary expression of the sex-instinct in the interests of humanity as a whole. This ordinary expression of the sex-instinct is, of course, the mating of man and woman. That there are other expressions of the instinct is self-evident; and many of these also can be directed so as to minister to the well-being of the race. The time is past when voluntary celibacy in all its forms came under universal condemnation in Protestant circles. It is recognized to-day that those who accept the monastic vocation with a pure desire to serve God and man to the best of their ability may well discover that the sex-instinct, so far from being repressed thereby and becoming a menace to personality, will find a new and sublimated channel of expression in sympathetic prayer or loving devotion to the needs of mankind. Others, again, find themselves debarred by domestic ties, by financial stringency, or other circumstances, from the sex-life to which matrimony has hitherto been the only door sanctioned by general civilized approval. In their case also, if the barriers are frankly accepted as insuperable, there is commonly no such psychical catastrophe as would suggest that the pent-up or thwarted sex-instinct must have its revenge. Somehow or

E

other it finds sufficient and healthful outlet in this case as in the former one. So the woman who has sacrificed her youth to the care of aged parents can solace herself, when 'freedom' comes, by devotion to social service; and even the neglected spinster, whose maternal sympathies go out to nothing more important than a parrot or a Pekinese, finds a relative tranquillity for herself, and does no great injury to society.

These, however, are not what we have called the 'ordinary' expressions of the sex-instinct. It is with the latter we are concerned—with that activity which a great authority classed among the four things 'too wonderful' for him—more aspiring than the way of an eagle in the air; more sinuous than the way of a serpent on a rock; more purposeful than the way of a ship in the midst of the sea—the way of a man with a maid. But in considering the problem here presented to us we do not start *in vacuo*. A great tradition already holds the field, or has done so until very recent times. This is the tradition of Christian civilization, especially as it has operated in Europe, and so has affected the social and domestic outlook of Western nations. The tradition in question can easily be summarized. It holds that the best interests of humanity at large will be promoted if, in general, the only type of sex-union to which social approval is given is one set in the context of a deliberate and voluntary *consortium* of interests, goods, and family life, undertaken with all the solemnity of a public contract, and with the fullest possible intention of permanence on either side. It is an obvious truth that neither legislation (whether ecclesiastical or civil), nor custom, nor convention can *make* any one moral. Nevertheless these influences do beyond question move the thoughts of men and women in the directions to which they point; hence it seems in the main appropriate (so the tradition would say) that legislation, custom, and convention alike should refuse to approve any change of partners during the lifetime of a couple so united— should forbid, in fact, 'remarriage after divorce'.

It is recognized, of course, that these legislative articulations of the tradition have never been utterly merciless. Such a weakening of the *consortium* as is involved in what is nowadays known as 'legal' or 'judicial separation' has always been treated as valid where the cause has been grave enough. In addition, Christendom both Eastern and Western has always admitted something not unlike divorce with the right of remarriage in specified types of case. But these mitigations of severity have been treated throughout as exceptions—and, indeed, undesirable exceptions— to the principle at stake. They have been necessitated by faulty social conditions and the 'hardness of men's hearts'. They are declensions from the ideal, to be kept in check as much as possible in a world which is very far from being made up of perfect men and women.

The first step, therefore, is obviously to ask, 'How has this tradition worked?' Here at once we meet with divergent judgements. It is convenient to give each of them a name for purposes of reference; but we must be careful to avoid question-begging designations. The names I choose, therefore, are chosen for convenience only; they are not intended at this stage to indicate either approval or disapproval. Let us say that we can distinguish three separate answers to the question we have put—the Realist, the Pessimist, and the Romanticist answer respectively.

(1) The Realist answer to the question, 'How has the general Christian tradition worked in the matter of sex?' is quite definitely, 'Not at all badly on the whole'. Civilization, the Realist says, might have gone a good deal farther and fared a great deal worse. He recognizes, of course, that many marriages have been or are unhappy ones; that there is always the possibility of differences of opinion and taste, of jealousies and petty quarrels; of those breakfast-table amenities which lend colour to the hope that the Recording Angel does not come on duty before nine o'clock in the morning. Nevertheless, he says, the unhappy marriages are not sufficient in number to warrant anything so violent as the abolition of the traditional system and the introduction of a new and altogether untried one. Many of the marriages which are admittedly failures can be dealt with by one or other of the safety valves to which we have alluded; in the remaining cases we must ask the unfortunate persons concerned to be content with such mitigations as are possible, and for the rest to steel themselves to suffer for the good of society as a whole.

(2) The Pessimist view is the direct opposite of that which we have called the Realist. Surveying the whole field of human marriage, the Pessimist decides that he cannot call to mind any institution which has been less successful in achieving its purpose. He magnifies every occasion of dispute, however trivial, between the spouses, until it becomes a veritable *casus belli*; he scents irremediable tragedy behind even those unions which offer the most convincing outward appearance of marital happiness. This universal unhappiness of the married he attributes to all kinds of causes—incompatibility of temper, ill health, unpunctuality, slovenliness, indifferent household management and catering and cooking by the wife, miserliness in domestic expenditure by the husband, and so forth. Yet he does not consciously plead for the inauguration of a new system. *In principle* he stands by the tradition. He would *like* all marriages to be lifelong, but so long as men and women are what they are he sees little hope of maintaining this view in practice. Consequently, he pleads for an almost indefinite extension of the safety valves, and insists that cheap and easy divorce on a scale approximating to that in force in some states of the American Union is the only solution for our difficulties.

(3) The Romanticist (who, curiously enough, claims also to speak as a psychologist) agrees neither with the Realist nor the Pessimist. The former, he claims, has failed to recognize the symptoms; the latter has given a false diagnosis of the disease. The present

system, he holds, is indeed profoundly unsatisfactory
—so unsatisfactory, in short, that nothing less than a
revolution will suffice to put matters right. But its
unsatisfactoriness cannot be traced to those minor
causes of rupture which the Pessimist has enumerated.
The root of the difficulty is sex, and no solution which
fails to grasp this truth will be more than a superficial
palliative. Sex, the Romanticist says, is a clamant and
masterful instinct; it must have its way; and the
tragedy of modern marriage is that only rarely does
it represent the mating of a couple harmoniously
sexed. When the one is passionate, the other is cold
and listless; when the one is sensitive and shrinking,
the other is rough and boisterous. The root cause of
matrimonial unhappiness, therefore, is 'sexual maladjustment'.

We must pause for a moment to notice the extra-
ordinarily elusive character of the evidence on which
these very different conclusions are based. In England it is garnered by observation and experience
alone; in America it is reached by the *questionnaire*
method in addition. A series of inquiries, for example, will be addressed to 'a group of one hundred
and sixteen unhappily married women', 'asking them
to give the reasons for their unhappiness'; and, even
where the results scarcely bear out the principle which
the inquirer is hoping to establish, it is always possible
for him to say that the witnesses were 'unable accu-
rately to diagnose their psychological reactions',[1] and

¹ Cp. J. P. Lichtenberger, *Divorce*, pp. 382, 383.

then to give his own diagnosis untrammelled even by the very statistics to which he has appealed. With methods such as these, it will be evident, an interesting variety of conclusions can be reached.

The real point at issue, however, is not the empirical question 'What percentage of marriages under the existing system can be called "happy", or "satisfactory", or "socially beneficial"?' On the available evidence it would be impossible to maintain that any answer to this question could be relied upon as even approximately true to the facts. The real problem is a deeper one. It puts the question, 'What is the psychological importance of sex in relation to human conduct?' This would appear at first sight to be a question capable of scientific investigation, as the other is not; but even here we notice that the accuracy of the answer depends upon the correct assembling of the evidence, and, *the evidence being the same as before*, it remains as elusive as ever. No doubt the psychologist will say that he has an abundant array of facts on which to base his conclusion; but once again we may inquire whether sufficient weight has been attached to the overwhelming number of marriages which (just because they are relatively 'happy') never come under his notice. Fortunately for our purpose, however, we shall find it unnecessary to enter upon any discussion of this point. We may content ourselves by noticing the degree to which the different answers diverge.

To the Realist and the Pessimist alike, sex is a

normal biological instinct, not differing very greatly
from any other instinct. It has periods of intense and
it may be prolonged activity, during which it can easily
achieve a marked dominance over the other instincts.
Happily for the human race, however, it has other
periods when it is relatively dormant, and makes little
if any claim for satisfaction. Above all, it may be
described as a *robust* or *virile* instinct : in the ordinary
man or woman it can within limits be checked,
thwarted, disciplined, without any grave fear of serious consequences. This, the Realist says, is the reason
why the Christian tradition has on the whole worked
well. The tradition does indeed demand a considerable limitation of the sex-instinct, but the instinct is
capable of standing the strain. So no harm is done by
the demand for chastity outside marriage, and self-
control within; whilst the good resulting in other
ways from a monogamous system is obvious. And
though the Pessimist, of course, does not associate
himself with this cheerful estimate of the Christian
tradition as a whole, he does at least claim that the
view of sex just indicated corroborates, and in its turn
is corroborated by, the fact that there are very many
other causes of unhappy marriages beside 'sexual maladjustment'.

The Romantic view, however, though it commonly
appeals for support to the most modern and advanced
psychological theories, is really a throwback to earlier
times—the times of the troubadours, for example, or
of the Greek erotic novelists, or even of Sappho. On

this view, sex stands virtually alone among the instincts, both by reason of its urgency, and by reason of its sensitiveness. The latter characteristic is the more important of the two. The urgency of sexual desires would not in itself present mankind with a problem *sui generis*; but such a problem is created by their supposed sensitiveness. For we are now told that, so far from the instinct being 'robust' and 'virile', it is the most delicate of machines, and needs the most expert handling. Maltreat or abuse it to the slightest degree (and by maltreating and abusing the Romanticist means what ordinary men would call 'self-control') and the result may be too terrible to contemplate. From the cradle to the grave—so runs this most popular of psychological creeds—man is above all else a creature of sex; and if his particular sex-conditionings are not properly satisfied we have no reason to be either shocked or surprised at any abnormalities that may ensue.

Clearly, if this is the truth about the psychology of sex, we have the most cogent *a priori* grounds for arguing that the Christian tradition *must* be adjudged a failure. For any system which demands such constant and consistent discipline of the sex-instinct as does that tradition is so unsound that all the observed miseries of married life can reasonably be set down to its account; and if at first sight we cannot observe as many of these miseries as so unnatural a system seems bound to produce, we may fairly assume that there are in fact innumerable cases which have only failed to come to light because of the natural reluctance of men and women to reveal their most intimate troubles to the world at large. But, fortunately, as we have already observed, it is unnecessary to go into this vexed question of evidence. For not only will it appear that the Romanticist's proposals for solving the problem suffer from all the defects of which he accuses the Christian tradition. We may go farther, and assert that he imports into his solution conditions which would make a satisfactory issue utterly impossible. Judged on the ground of mere self-consistency, the Romanticist's palliatives are impotent to secure their purpose—they transcend the limits within which alone he allows a solution to be looked for, as frankly as does (in his opinion) the conservative tradition itself.

What, then, does the Romanticist ask? Let it be clear at once that our concern is not with those who either by literary insinuation or by active propaganda plead for complete promiscuity in matters of sex. Nor are we concerned with proposals which could only be realized after the entire social framework had been refashioned on a completely new model. We confine ourselves to the published views of writers who, whilst profoundly dissatisfied with things as they are, and deeply imbued with the new psychology of sex, put forward their proposals with a genuine sense of responsibility as practical and constructive measures which might well be adopted here and now to ease

what they conceive to be the existing tension. And
from the outset it becomes apparent that on three
points at least the Romanticist solution (within the
limits which such responsible writers themselves set
for it) speaks with the same voice as tradition:

(1) First of all, it frowns upon anything akin to
promiscuity, libertinism, or mere sexual adventur-
ousness. The new sex-relationships which it seeks to
introduce form a system; and it would have this
system at once recognized and controlled by society,
with the sanction of general disapproval, if not of
penal legislation, held in reserve for use against those
who overstep its bounds. Thus, though it may claim
that the discipline of the sex-instinct which it seeks
to impose is less frankly uncongenial than that of
the Christian code, it remains a discipline none
the less; and those who find their ideal in complete
and undisciplined licence will never be at home
with it.

(2) In the second place, it puts a premium on
parenthood where possible. Quite why this is so it
is difficult to discover. The 'new morality' to which
the Romantic school adheres is a morality of happiness rather than of duty; and it does not as a rule
advocate the responsibility of nurturing, clothing,
educating, and providing for a family as one of the
most obvious routes to individual enjoyment. There
is always, therefore, a certain reticence or elusiveness
in the argument at this point; we are almost led to
suspect that a link in the chain has been omitted (with

the hope that the omission will go unperceived) because of some exceptional incongruity which its frank recognition would bring to light. But we are entitled to press for an answer. Why, we may ask, should the Romanticist, after emancipating himself from so many of the shibboleths of traditional ethics, still wish to prohibit what the old-fashioned moralist used to call 'race-suicide'? Is it that, despite all his modernism, he is still under the influence of that naïve nineteenth-century creed which regarded the 'maintenance of the population' as a duty laid upon society by some mystic principle of Evolution? Or are we to credit him with a pathological craving for seeing mankind in the mass —a phobia of a world so empty that the exhilarating spectacles of a European war, a Bank Holiday mob at a London terminus, or the myriads of football enthusiasts at Wembley or at Twickenham, would never again be possible? It is for the Romanticist to say on what grounds he shrinks from any alliance with those more casual minds which would taste all the pleasures of sex without incurring the penalty (as it seems to them) of a family.

Nevertheless, we may perhaps be allowed to present him with an argument which he himself is curiously slow to use. The old prophet, when he predicted the glories of the restored Jerusalem that was to be, put as its crowning beauty the promise that 'the streets of the city shall be full of boys and girls playing in the streets thereof'. Here is an ideal whose force none but the most hardened and cynical of worldlings

will deny. The prospect of a world without children
—a world progressively deprived, or depriving itself,
of the innocent joys, laughter, and enthusiasms of a
younger generation, continually pressing forward to
be, not merely an embarrassment, but far more a tonic
and a solace to the middle-aged and elderly—is a
prospect which very few would care to face with
equanimity. And if this is so, then none but the most
narrowly anti-social of egotists can deny that for the
well-being of society as a whole, if not also for his own
personal happiness, it is incumbent on him, in planning out what may be called his sex-life, to include the
procreation of children and the responsibilities of
parenthood as duties falling within its scope. This is
not by any means to say that a return to the almost un-
restricted child-bearing of the Victorian era is right or
desirable under modern conditions—that is a wholly
different question. It is merely to assert, as part of the
sober Romanticist creed, that the irresponsible though
determined attempt of the profligate (whether male
or female) to enjoy the pleasures of sex whilst exclud-
ing all possibility of parenthood, is a crime against
society.

(3) The third point on which Romanticism agrees
with the Christian tradition is that, once parenthood
has supervened upon mating, the care of the children
becomes the paramount duty of both parents. This
means that, unless and until the whole framework of
Western civilization is revolutionized, the normal
family in which there are children must conform to

the ideal of a permanent monogamous household, at all events until the children have been launched upon their independent careers. For, short of a universalized system of State mating and breeding, under which the Government would take over the entire charge of infants from the moment of birth, it is agreed that the family unit must remain in being; and that for this to be possible monogamy and permanence must still be the rule. 'My own view', wrote Mr. Bertrand Russell on one occasion, 'is that the state and the law should take no notice of sexual relations apart from children. ... But when once there are children, I think that divorce should be avoided except for a very grave cause. ... A home with two parents is best for children. I do not feel that the main thing in marriage is the feeling of the parents for each other; the main thing is co-operation in bearing children.'[1] 'The normal environment of children,' says another writer, 'and that best adapted to their training and to the most successful adjustment of their behaviour reactions to their social group in the interests of good citizenship, is the happy well-ordered home, in which both parents co-operate helpfully to further these desirable ends.'[2] Such 'happy well-ordered homes', we may add, are far more likely to be maintained under a system which, by refusing to the parents the opportunity of divorce on grounds of trivial disagreement or of a passing desire for another and more attractive alliance, instils

[1] Quoted in W. Lippmann, *Preface to Morals*, p. 299.
[2] J. P. Lichtenberger, *Divorce*, p. 139.

in them the conviction that their duty is to make the best of the existing marriage, and subordinate their own interests to those of the children.

To put this creed in a nutshell we may say that Romanticism follows tradition at all events to the extent of insisting (i) that mere sexual promiscuity is wholly to be deplored and condemned; (ii) that every healthy male and female in society should regard it as a *prima facie* duty at some period in his or her life to aim at parenthood; and (iii) that, where parenthood has been achieved, parents must maintain a relatively stable monogamous partnership, at all events until the children have been launched upon their careers, since otherwise the household will disintegrate with consequences unfavourable to the upbringing of the younger generation.

As a first comment upon this view, and before we proceed to notice the points at which Romanticism differs from tradition, we may observe that it demands of the individual a very high degree of self-discipline in the matter of sex. Even if he is not a parent he must not regard himself as at liberty to indulge in haphazard sexual intercourse; he is to remember that he is a man and not a beast. Further, he is called upon to consider seriously the duty of maintaining the race; and if he embarks upon this task (as normally he would seem required to do), and in the course of nature is rewarded with success, he must then for a period of perhaps twenty years put an even greater restraint upon any wayward tendency he may have to exchange his partner for another and more alluring one. If we remember that Romanticism claims a basis in psychology, and particularly in that psychology which regards the yoke of Christian monogamy as too severe for the sexual impulses of the normal man or woman, we may well ask whether even the mitigations allowed by this new system are sufficient to eliminate the dangers of inhibition and repression which we are told attend every serious restraint of sex. Certainly the libertine will not think so; the compromise offered him by the Romantic will prove little more attractive than the rigour of the Christian code. This is a serious criticism : for a compromise which satisfies none but a tiny minority is a poor substitute for a system which, whatever its defects, has at all events proved a very remarkable influence for good in the progress of civilization, social stability, and good manners.

But we have not so far considered the positive demands of the 'new morality' in the matter of sex. They may be summarized under two headings; and it will simplify matters if from this stage forward we use the word 'marriage' (without qualifying adjective) for any sex-union undertaken with the hope of offspring. Expressed in terms of this usage, the Romantic demands are as follows :

(i) That so long as a 'marriage' (though undertaken with the hope of children) proves childless, or (where children have been born) when they no longer need their parents' care and oversight, the partners to a union shall have the right to divorce on the easiest possible grounds, with (of course) the right of entering into new unions.

(ii) That adolescents who for good reason (as, for example, lack of means or of continuous employment) would be unwise as yet to undertake the responsibilities of parenthood, should in the meantime be allowed a considerable degree of liberty in 'sex experimentation' (often called 'companionate' or 'trial marriage'), with the use of 'scientific methods of birth control' to avoid the procreation of children; it being understood that while, on the one hand, any such childless 'companionate marriage' could be dissolved on easy terms at will, the parties to it should, on the other hand, exhibit due fidelity to one another during its continuance, so as to avoid the danger of its degenerating into a mere cloak for promiscuity.

Once more we notice, in this second demand, the recognition that a greater degree of self-discipline in sex is necessary than the profligate would ever be willing to exercise over himself. It is unnecessary to repeat the obvious criticism made only a few paragraphs ago; what is more important, at the present stage, is to notice that this fact endows the proposals under consideration with a sobriety which should at least win for them respectful attention. The ill-founded outburst of criticism which has so often greeted the very mention of 'companionate marriage', since Judge Lindsey first gave the phrase currency, is in large part due to complete and culpable failure to recognize that

the proposals associated with the words are an attempt
to cure the actual evils of the day—the wanton, pagan,
and widespread playing with sex-impulse by adolescents of which Judge Lindsey believed himself to
have convincing proof—by inaugurating a régime of
relative self-discipline, and not a signal and manifest
triumph of cynical immoralism over all the canons
of modesty and decency. We may disapprove of the
proposals in question as much as we wish—we may find
overwhelming reasons for regarding them as wholly
impracticable, whether praiseworthy or the reverse;
but there is no doubt whatever that the motives which
lie behind them are such as every serious-minded person must commend. They are at all events a genuine
attempt to solve a difficult problem, not a cutting of
the Gordian knot.

What is to be said then of these two Romanticist
demands? Let us take the question of divorce first
of all. Here in general, divorce with the right of remarriage, as distinct from judicial separation, appears
to be denied to all but childless couples (or those
whose children have reached maturity) except perhaps for very grave cause. This is Earl Russell's view,
and he adds explicitly: 'I should not regard physical
infidelity as a very grave cause'[1]—thus introducing a
limitation more severe than any recognized by the
English Courts of to-day. Such a solution can satisfy
no one; indeed it stultifies itself. One of the primary

[1] Quoted by Lippmann, p. 298.

aims of the Romanticist is to stimulate parenthood.
Parenthood has its joys, but it has its cares as well;
and it is notorious that many couples are already so
afraid of these cares that they prefer to remain childless. The married couple with a family of children,
they say, is unduly handicapped in the search for happiness. But the Romanticist proposes to handicap
them even further. Hitherto, we may say, the public
conscience has demanded the payment of a price for
sexual experience (the price, namely, of entering upon
a lifelong tie); whilst a further price (that of parental
cares) must be paid by those whose union issues in
children. But the Romanticist now proposes, in effect,
to make sexual experience free to all; and to demand
both prices of those, and only those, who accept the
responsibility of parenthood which he urges upon
them. The result will inevitably be to stimulate that
tendency to childless unions which he himself de-
plores. In this, as in everything else, it is of course
the case that those who take their duties seriously will
always be at a disadvantage as compared with those
who do not; and the task of the wise legislator is so
to adjust the balance as to induce the irresponsible
to listen to the call of duty by penalizing them if they
will not do so. But the Romanticist is taking the
opposite course. He would allow those who refuse
the obligation of parenthood an additional advantage (as it will seem to them) which they do not at
present possess—the advantage, namely, of a freedom to transfer their affections to new partners at

will; whilst at the same time he introduces no mitigation for those who accept the vocation of parenthood. The Christian tradition will agree with him wholeheartedly in this latter particular; but as regards the former it will say, with justice, that he is proposing a course disastrous not only to traditional ideals, but to his own as well.

Thus, if extended facilities for divorce are to be allowed at all they must be allowed to all—there must be no unequal discrimination in favour of the childless. Here we find ourselves face to face with the Pessimist once more; but we come to meet him with certain principles in our possession of which our study of Romanticism has made us aware.

The first is that, in any marriage which has resulted in children, *the welfare of the children is the consideration of primary importance*; the second that, in general, *this welfare will best be promoted where facilities for divorce are restricted as much as possible*. The welfare of the children demands that wherever possible parents shall adjust such difficulties and disagreements (whether great or small) as may arise between them, in order to maintain the integrity of the family unit; and obviously the best stimulus towards such adjustment, in the case of the ordinary man and woman, will be the knowledge that no other way of escape lies open. The welfare of the children, again, demands that neither parent should allow his or her interest to stray away from the family unit with a view to forming a new alliance elsewhere; and this end will be best secured if it is known that society will not tolerate any such change of alliance.

The conclusion is obvious. However much we may sympathize with hard cases, and whatever exceptional expedients we may allow for mitigating their worst severities, the general well-being of the nation's childhood demands a reinforcement rather than a relaxation of the ideal of the permanent monogamous household; and only those who think more of satisfying the selfish interests of the adult than of maintaining that healthy family atmosphere which is essential to the true happiness and development of the child can seriously advocate any other view. All marriages must be treated alike, the childless with the fertile. In the case of the latter, it is vital for the children's sake that grounds of divorce should be refused in all but the most extreme circumstances; the same principle therefore must be observed in the case of the former.

The case for 'companionate' or 'trial marriage', with deliberate intent to avoid parenthood at all events for the time being, *and with the right to divorce at will so long as there are no children*, is obviously no more than a plea that concubinage should be generally recognized as unobjectionable for the young, as a temporary outlet for their sex-life until they reach an economic position in which parenthood will not be incompatible with prudence, and discover a partner with whom a life-long marriage will not be intolerable. The sensuous and rhetorical language in which this plea is so often couched need not concern us, nor need we (for our present purposes) do more than glance at the horror which it is bound to excite in any one who has the Christian view of sex in reverence. The gist of any criticism to which such proposals are subjected may well be that once more the Romanticist is trying to combine two contradictory purposes, and that once more he has signally failed.

I have pointed out elsewhere[1] that the view of marriage which includes parenthood within its scope, and (where parenthood is achieved) makes the children's well-being the primary responsibility of father and mother, is essentially one in which the sex-life is regarded as a *vocation*. On the other hand, any view which tolerates sexual intercourse in which the possibility of offspring is prohibited is a view which treats the sex-life, if not as that mere sale and purchase of favours which we call prostitution, at all events as a *recreation*. Nothing in this distinction prevents us from saying that the happiest marriages combine both aspects, and are at once recreative (that is, sources of continual joy to the parents) and vocational. But it remains true of sex as of anything else, that the more it is treated exclusively as a means of recreation the more difficult it will be to regard it at a later stage as a vocation. This is the principle which the Romanticist ignores. For a period of ten or fifteen years from adolescence he will permit, and indeed encourage, the young man or young woman to regard sex as purely

[1] *Marriage and Divorce*, pp. 112–121.

recreative; thereafter he demands of them that (if economic conditions allow) they shall embark upon the
responsibility of parenthood, and subordinate their
sex-instinct for the next twenty or twenty-five years
wholly to the vocation of bringing up their children
in the harmonious atmosphere of a monogamous
household. And obviously such a complete *volte face*
is more than human nature can endure, especially if
sex is the ravenous instinct which the Romanticists
affirm it to be.

The truth of this criticism may be made clear by a
very simple analogy. Consider a child brought up in
a house full of books. He is told, no doubt, that in
fifteen years' time he will have to treat the books seriously, read them, and master their contents. But in
the meantime he is at liberty to do with them as he
will: to use them as bricks for building, as missiles for
hurling, as make-believe boats to float in his bath; to
tear out their pages to be folded into paper darts or
hats or aeroplanes. It seems unlikely that such a régime carried out continuously and uninterruptedly
for many years during the most formative period of
life will fit a child for assuming in due course the
responsibilities, let us say, of Bodley's librarian. His
ingrained conviction that books are no more than
toys would be too strong even for the sobering influences of his new position. Or, if this instance is
thought to be too imaginative, we may take an example from actual life. For four hundred years or so
the 'white' races have learnt to treat the 'coloured'

as their toys—as 'lesser breeds without the law', possessed of only the sketchiest of rights—as something little better than animals, to be enslaved, exploited, or exterminated as may be most convenient. We are alive now to the fatally un-Christian character of any such view; but contemporary history is not lacking in evidence which proves how difficult the white races find it to assimilate the obvious truth that colour has nothing to do with rights, and that all men are equal in the sight of God. The older view has sunk too deeply into the grain. 'Once a toy always a toy' seems, in fact, to be the rule of the world; and to treat sex as a game is the least reasonable way of preparing for treating it as a vocation. The battle of Waterloo may have been won on the playing fields of Eton, but the carpet knights of companionate marriage will show themselves poor soldiers when they face the stern demands of parenthood.

In the matter of divorce it is conceivable, at least, that a compromise between the Romantic and the Christian tradition might be discovered which would not be unworkable. Their aims, after all, are identical; even the Romantic hopes that every companionate marriage will turn into a real marriage in time, and so will conform to the monogamous pattern. And the Christian, for his part, recognizes that divorce legislation, whether ecclesiastical or civil, is a means and not an end; so that if some relaxation of the existing code could be shown to offer good hope of fostering the acceptance of the Christian ideal throughout

society, no objection could be raised in principle.
Severity is not always the surest method of securing
conformity; and the uncompromising translation of
a principle into a legal enactment sometimes alienates
more minds than it reconciles. But in the matter of companionate marriage the two points of view involved
are manifestly incompatible; and our main criticism
of the Romanticist is that, so far from seeing this, he
regards the transition from the one to the other, when
circumstances call for it, as the easiest process imagin-
able. To such a view experience opposes an absolute *non possumus*. On this head we must say that the
Romanticist proposes to us a compromise which is
frankly preposterous. There can be no half-way house
between frank libertinism and the Christian view of
sex. The system which the Romanticist favours is no
more than an idle day-dream belonging at best to that
amoral and fantastic world of the Comedy of Manners for which Charles Lamb has said all that can be
said, but condemned by its own inherent inconsis-
tencies to immediate and utter failure the moment
any attempt be made to put it into practice.

III. PATRIOTISM

By JOHN P. R. MAUD

WHAT is patriotism? Dr. Johnson defines the patriot in his dictionary as 'one whose ruling passion is the love of his country'; and Boswell says of a pamphlet which Johnson wrote, that 'it contained an admirable display of the properties of a real patriot, in the original and genuine sense:—a sincere, steady, rational, and unbiased friend to the interests and prosperity of his King and country'. However, in the dictionary Johnson has added a quotation from Addison which might have struck him as implying a rather different conception of patriotism from his own:

> The firm patriot there,
> Who made the welfare of mankind his care.

On the basis of these quotations we can say that the ethical problem involved in patriotism is the problem of how the man whose ruling passion is a love of his country can be so rational and unbiased a friend to his country's interests, that he makes not only the welfare of his country but the welfare of mankind his care; in other words, how the citizen of one nation can love other nations as he loves his own. There are, in fact, two aspects of this problem, the internal and the external (we may call them): my duty towards my neighbour in my own country, and my duty towards my neighbour in other countries. But the problem is a single one, and neither aspect can be properly considered except as complementary to the other. Burke's words have here a certain relevance: 'It is therefore our business carefully to cultivate in our minds, to rear to the most perfect vigour and maturity, every sort of generous and honest feeling that belongs to our nature. To bring the dispositions that are lovely in private life into the service and conduct of the commonwealth; so to be patriots as not to forget we are gentlemen.'[1]

Many people would say that this is frankly impossible; that to love my country as a patriot I must suppress all the generous and honest feelings which prompt me to consider the welfare of men in other countries than my own; and that therefore there is no ethical problem involved in patriotism except that of behaving justly towards my own countrymen. Other people would argue from the same premiss that the ethical problem of patriotism is so simple as not to need argument; my plain duty is to refuse the claim of my country point-blank, since to allow that claim means necessarily to fail in my duty to all the neighbours who happen not to live in my own country. In order to decide whether one or other of these assumptions ought to be made, something must first be said in answer to the general question: What conception of the nature and purpose of man ought we to have, when we consider men and nations as they are in twentieth-century Europe?

[1] *Thoughts on the Cause of the Present Discontents.*

Men are unique individuals; at any given moment each man is to some extent self-conscious, wanting certain things in a certain order of preference, and having a certain power of satisfying those wants, a power limited partly by the inherited and acquired capabilities of the individual, partly by his environment. But at the same time men are mutually in need of one another; and though all have something in common, divergences of want, capacity, and environment account for the fact that men are found everywhere in groups, which have come into existence, and continue, for innumerable reasons and in every variety of form. Families, cities, nations, federations, economic and social classes, political parties, churches, colleges, and clubs, are all the result of man's social character. Moreover, owing to the nature of some of their wants, men are constantly found in a state of conflict, both as individuals and as groups.

The assumption which a moral philosopher has to make is that there are certain capacities which the individual *ought* to develop, and a certain relationship to his neighbour in which he *ought* to stand. It follows then that a man has certain duties as a member of each group to which he belongs, and that each group can therefore be said to have a duty. It is no doubt true that men are even less likely to be what they ought to be, or do what they ought to do, as members of a group than as individuals. But if it be assumed that men as individuals have specific duties of their own, then as members of a group they must also have duties. Man's duty as the citizen of a state is a duty of this kind, though in certain respects, as will be seen later, different from any other kind of duty. The moral philosopher must assume that men as members of political groups, whether local, national, federal, or imperial, have duties, just as they have in respect of their membership of other groups; and he can therefore say that all these political groups have their own peculiar duties, which *ought* to determine their nature and actions. Whenever (for instance) a conflict arises between groups within a state or between two states, it *ought* to be decided according to some principle of justice, and not by a simple trial of strength by the conflicting parties. The patriot then has a duty on all such occasions, to bring it about, so far as he can, that the principle of justice relevant to the particular circumstances shall be discovered and acted upon.

But the question remains, are international disputes capable of resolution on just principles, so long as the existing organization (and lack of organization) of the world and the nation-state remains unchanged? Must the patriot who genuinely desires the discovery and doing of justice in the world do his best to forget his patriotism and induce other people to forget theirs? The answer depends partly on our conception of the nature of justice and partly on our view of the actual state of the world to-day. And our conception of justice—of the principle (that is to say) on which society ought to be organized,

and on which incidentally disputes ought to be decided—depends ultimately on the assumptions we
make concerning man's potentialities and the end
which he ought to seek. We may sum up the
assumptions that we intend to make by saying, first,
that man has a will which is capable of freedom and
is not necessarily the slave of the economic, social,
or political environment; and, secondly, that man
is capable of distinguishing among various possible
courses of action the one which he *ought* to follow
—that is to say, of recognizing his duty, whether or
not he wants to do it. Thirdly, his ultimate ideal is
to want to do what he ought to do: as the Christian
says, 'to love the thing which Thou commandest
and desire that which Thou dost promise'. Only in
so far as he achieves this identification of the will
as it is with the will as it ought to be can he enjoy
fullness of life.

Fourthly, the nature of the good life is such that
each man's duty as an individual is complementary
to his neighbour's: it can, in fact, be described as the
duty of loving his neighbour as himself; and there is
no human creature, in any part of the world, who may
not come into relationship with him as a neighbour.
When a man wills as he ought, he wills a whole which
includes his own interest and the interest of all men.
It perhaps invariably happens that at this, and all other
stages of history which precede the realization of the
ideal, even a perfectly good man would find that what
might be called his personal interest, conceived in

terms of what he *wants*, must be sacrificed; but this sacrifice can be freely willed, as being the only way in which under the circumstances the good life can be lived to the full.

Fifthly, if groups were as they ought to be and acted as they ought to act, there would similarly be no possibility of conflict. This, on the face of it, is a bolder assumption than the last; for, it may be said, 'we have had experience of one man sacrificing himself freely for his friends, and we know that where relationships are personal it is quite possible that no conflicts of interest will arise. But the relationship of group to group is impersonal; not only has there never been a recorded occasion on which a group voluntarily surrendered any part of its own interest, but in the nature of things such an event could never happen; for a group exists to get something done, and if it sacrificed its interest it would thereby fail in its purpose; on the other hand, the individual who sacrifices his interest may be said to succeed in the purpose he has as a human person.'

But the fact surely is that no group is more than one aspect of the men and women who are its members. The purpose of some groups is no doubt such that what the groups ought to do is to cease to exist; but there seems to be no *a priori* reason why a group should not be such that its purpose is to serve, in some particular way, the common purpose of humanity. A group of this kind would find on certain occasions that its duty was to sacrifice some part of what previously it had conceived to be the object of its existence, just as the individual constantly finds that his duty is to make a sacrifice; and to do this would not be the 'death' of the group, but the realization of its proper purpose. When states, which have hitherto been sovereign within their respective territories, decide to form a federation and relinquish some part of their local sovereignty in consequence, they may be acting under what they imagine to be the compulsion of circumstances, but their action nevertheless suggests the possibility that even national groups can modify their separate purposes and resign certain of their privileges, for the sake of a larger purpose which they choose to pursue in common, without ceasing to exist as individual states. But whether or not an act worthy of the name of voluntary sacrifice has ever been performed by a group, the assumption must be made that groups have a duty to make sacrifices under certain circumstances, and that it ought to be the purpose of every group to seek its particular end not as an end in itself but as part of that larger end which is the proper object of all human endeavour.

It follows from these assumptions that if people, as individuals and as members of groups, did as they *ought*, they would agree, and the groups would agree, about the common end which all in their various ways were seeking, and no one would be compelled against his will either to do or abstain from any course of action. On the other hand, it does *not* follow that each man's tastes or capacities would be the same;[1] nor that groups, with particular interests and characteristics, would cease to exist; nor that, in the process of gradually reaching agreement about the nature of the common end and of achieving it, there would not be need of force and the compulsion of the wills both of groups and individuals.

Then how much can the state be expected to help or to hinder man in his efforts to do his duty? The nature of the state has varied from age to age and from place to place; and even if attention is confined to a particular state at a particular time, it will be found that no two individuals either suffer or benefit in precisely the same way from it. However, there are perhaps four characteristics which the modern state always has. It is, in the first place, a group of which all those living within certain territorial limits are members, whether they like it or not. A characteristic of most other societies is that so long as a man is a member he must submit himself to the rules, but that he can resign if he objects to the rules or if for any other reason he no longer wishes to be a member. But any one who finds himself, by the accident of

[1] Contrast Plato, *Republic*, Bk. 5, 464*d* (Lindsay's translation): 'These regulations will . . . prevent the disruption of the city which would result if each called a different wife and different children his own, and thus implanted in the city the individual pleasures and griefs of individuals. Rather they will have one single belief concerning what is their own and be all concerned in the same purpose, and so will be, as far as possible, simultaneously affected by pleasure and pain (ὁμοπαθεῖς λύπης τε καὶ ἡδονῆς).'

birth or residence, a member of the group which is
called the state, can only 'contract out' of the obligations placed on him as a citizen by going away to
another country, or being sent to gaol, or escaping
the notice of the authorities.

Secondly, the state exists for certain purposes
which are various and always subject to change.
Security from the possible attack of other nations
and from certain (but not all) forms of arbitrary exploitation at the hands of one's own countrymen is at
present always one of the services which a state seeks
to provide; but there are no limits which can be de-
fined *a priori* to the efforts which a state might make to
increase the health, wealth, or happiness of its citizens.
At any given moment the purposes for which the
state exists can (in theory, at any rate) be known by
any one who knows the law of the land; with a large
part of the citizen's life the state is not concerned, and
the law leaves him free to do as he likes; but this law
is constantly being modified in the process of ad-
ministration, and can be altered, in whole or in part,
at any future moment. In this respect, it may be noted,
the modern state differs somewhat from the ancient.
In Aristotle's time it could be said that legislation
was merely the codification of custom, and frequent
changes in the law were deprecated on the ground
that they undermined the citizen's habit of obedience.[1] Again, at the time when the book which is
still the Prayer Book of the Church of England was

---

[1] Aristotle, *Politics*, ii. 8. 23.

first published, it was natural to sum up the prayer
for those who were responsible under the King for
the internal government of the country in these
words: 'And grant unto his [that is, the King's]
whole Council, and to all that are put in authority
under him, that they may truly and indifferently minister justice, to the punishment of wickedness and
vice, and to the maintenance of Thy true religion,
and virtue.'[1] The assumption was that those in authority knew what people should and what they should
not be allowed to do, that this was incorporated in
the law, and that the officers of the state had only to
punish the evil-doer and perhaps incidentally praise
the virtuous. Since that time it has come to be regarded as more doubtful what kinds of action are
wrong, and which of these the law can attempt to
prevent with any likelihood of success; and the law
has been developed more and more as an instrument
of social action.

The third characteristic of the state is closely bound
up with the two already mentioned. The state has at
its disposal a more or less unlimited amount of force,
which can be used if necessary (though the fact that
it can be used makes its actual use unnecessary as a

[1] Compare also i. Peter, ii. 13 (the passage read as special
Epistle in the Communion Service on the Anniversary of
the King's Accession), 'Submit yourselves to every ordinance
of man for the Lord's sake: whether it be to the King as
supreme; or unto governors, as unto them that are sent by
him for the punishment of evil-doers or for the praise of them
that do well.'

rule), to ensure that the citizens fulfil their obligations (in money and personal service, for instance) and abstain from any act (such as the commission of a nuisance) which the state forbids. This force is symbolized by the policeman; and it is distinguished from the arbitrary compulsion exercised by persons or groups other than the state by the fact that its application can (in theory, at least) be predicted, since it is used only in accordance with principles declared publicly in the law.

These are three of the principal features of the state considered from its internal aspect, that is, as it affects its own citizens. The fourth characteristic is seen in its external activities. One state meets another with the claim to a practically unqualified sovereignty, and purports to speak for the whole body of its own citizens. Consequently there is a striking contrast between the internal and external aspects of the modern state. Internally it is characterized (in theory at any rate) by the rule of law; all citizens share, whether they wish to share or not, in certain benefits and burdens, for which they have the state to bless or curse; there is machinery to determine what these benefits and burdens shall be, and to secure that the general intentions of the law are carried out in particular places, at particular times, and through particular persons; a system of judicial tribunals to determine any dispute that may arise when it is alleged that the law has been broken; and finally a police force to see that effect is given to the decision of the court. On the

other hand, if we consider the external relations of
one state to another, we find a condition of affairs
which might almost be described as anarchy or the rule
of lawlessness. It is true that an embryonic international organization exists in the League of Nations;
but in no sense can this be called a super-state. Only
those states belong who wish to belong, and every
state holds itself free to give notice of the termina-
tion of its membership. It bears a shadowy resem-
blance to the state in seeking to provide its members
with various services, concerned with certain aspects
of their health, wealth, and happiness. But security
it cannot hope to provide, so long as it is not granted
the same kind of monopoly which the nation-state
possesses for the provision of internal security, and
the same power to call on whatever police force it
thinks necessary. Meanwhile each state has to rely
on its own resources for securing itself against attack,
and naturally supplies itself with military force; this
increases the sense of insecurity in the mind of neigh-
bouring states, who take further thought for their
armaments, and so increase the general sense of insecurity. The nature of these military forces is sharply
distinguished from that of policemen, by the fact that
neither the system of international law nor the international machinery for deciding disputes is sufficient
to prevent a particular state from using its military
force in an effort to establish its own interpretation
of its own rights; whereas the police can only act in
accordance with the law, as declared in general terms

for the whole territory and interpreted in particular cases of dispute by a tribunal, which at least in theory is impartial.

Further, although the League is concerned with matters of health, trade, and so on, and for that side of its work can even count on the co-operation of states which are not members of the League, it cannot at present effect much in this direction except in such non-controversial subjects as research and information. When the states wish to find a common purpose and take common action in the more important spheres of economics or politics, they manufacture a special organization, which usually comes into being in the form of a conference, and passes away again when the absence of common purpose becomes too abundantly plain.

Such being the nature of the modern state, can any general answer be given to the question, how ought the state to be used or altered if man is to do his duty and eventually fulfil his proper purpose? It can be said at the outset that even if the laws of a state at any given time were in fact just (that is to say, as good as they could be, from the point of view of humanity as a whole), there would probably still be at least two disadvantages to be overcome. Some people, in the first place, would almost certainly think one or other of the laws unjust, and would have to choose between acting contrary to their conscientious conception of duty, or being punished for their disobedience. If we assume that these people would necessarily be

wrong in thinking any of the laws unjust, there is no
reason why this disadvantage should not in the end
be removed; for just laws must by their very nature
be *capable* of recognition as such by all people who do
as they ought. But it is important to notice that the
laws must not only *be* just, but be recognized as just,
if the good life is to be lived under them. It is just,
let us suppose, that the slum landlord who conscientiously objects to the Slum Clearance Acts should
have his property forcibly demolished; but it would
be better still if his conscience ceased to object.

Secondly, even those who recognized the justice
of the laws would be placed at a certain disadvantage
by the fact that compulsion could be put upon them
if they did not fulfil their legal obligations. Compare,
for instance, the man who voluntarily subscribes to a
hospital, with the man who would no less willingly
subscribe to such a purpose, but who, since he happens to live in a city where the hospitals are provided
by the municipality, makes his contribution in the
form of a tax, which he would be compelled to pay
even if he wished to do nothing of the kind. The
second man is likely to have quite different feelings
about the payment of a tax from those which he would
have, and which the first man has, about a voluntary
contribution. In the same way, when education or
the relief of the destitute has to be paid for out of
taxation, many, even of those who think the Education or Poor Law Acts just, make their compulsory
payments in a very different spirit from that in which

they would subscribe voluntarily to either of these purposes. This disadvantage is obviously capable of circumvention; for there is no reason why people should not come to regard the tax-collector as a public benefactor, who enables them to do what they want to do (that is, to love their neighbour) more efficiently than they could otherwise do, rather than as a highway robber who puts the pistol to their head.

The potential coercion of the law, then, lays a special obligation on those who recognize its justice, to obey it in a certain spirit and, by continuing to have a personal sense of responsibility for their neighbours and a spontaneous anxiety for their welfare, to neutralize the evil effect which just laws are in danger of producing even on those who recognize their justice. The actual coercion of those who break the law, not from conscientious scruple but knowing that they ought to obey it (the thief, for instance, who knows he should not steal, or the motorist who drives to the danger of the public), is of an entirely different kind, which has its peculiar disadvantages. Here the lawbreaker can fulfil his special obligation, perhaps, by accepting punishment or paying damages without resentment or sense of grievance.

But the question whether the state can hinder or help the living of the good life depends ultimately on the justice or injustice of the laws and policy of the state. It would be ridiculous to try to describe the characteristics by which a just law could be recognized; but two generalizations can be made at the outset. To be just, the laws or policy of a state must be in the interest of a particular country only in so far as that interest is part of the common interest of all persons concerned; in other words, they must seek a world purpose in general and a local purpose in particular. They may happen to be at the same time in the special interest of a particular person or group, of the majority or the minority of the citizens, of every one or of no one in a particular country; the benefits and burdens which they bring may be distributed evenly or unevenly, according to the circumstances of the place and time; but by none of these facts is the justice of the laws either constituted or destroyed. In other words, by saying that the laws are just or unjust, we do *not* mean that they are, or are not, what any one group or person wants them to be, nor do we mean that they are what the majority of the citizens, or even the whole complement of all the citizens, want them to be; we mean something which can be said in no other way than by saying that the laws are what they *ought* to be.

Secondly, we can say that the content of just laws at one time will almost certainly be different from the content of just laws at any other time. Formally they will always be the same; that is to say, they will at each stage be in the interest of humanity at large, and of a local community only in so far as that is consistent with the interest of the whole. But their substance at any one time will depend on the circumstances of that time and the living context within which they have to operate. They may be expected, then, to be continually changing as world-conditions change. Any attempt to draw up a set of just laws *a priori* without reference to a particular world-situation is therefore bound to be futile; and it is equally impossible to foretell what the duty of a citizen will be in relation to the state without full knowledge of the particular circumstances. Justice, in fact, is relative to the actual wants and experience of men, though it is not determined by them. It follows that the search for justice is not a search for a set of laws, which have been once for all laid up in heaven and might be recognized once for all by the political visionary on earth, but a continuous creative effort to discover from moment to moment what the purposes and methods of the state ought to be.

Two conditions must be satisfied if this search is to succeed. First, the maker of just laws must have knowledge of the facts; and this knowledge cannot be had (it seems) unless all the relevant experience of the men and women who would be affected by the laws (in all parts of the world) is made available: unless, that is to say, these men and women take some part in law-making. The philosopher-king of Plato's *Republic*, for example, could only be expected to perform his function of making just laws, if he could count on the co-operation of every one affected by them. Secondly, the law-maker must be disinterested; in judging what the law ought to be, he must disregard the benefits and burdens which he personally would receive in consequence of it. Those whose co-operation in law-making is required, because their experience has to be made available, must co-operate in a certain spirit and in a certain way; if they use the opportunity which participation in the work of legislation gives them to forward their particular personal interests, they can prevent the laws from being just; and this they will do, unless they regard their legislative function as a trust, and succeed in making their contribution as they *ought* to make it, from a disinterested desire to see justice done.

Obviously, therefore, it is not easy to make just laws; for they must be disinterested and at the same time based on knowledge which can only be given by those who will by the nature of the case find it most difficult to be disinterested. It seems right to conclude that no political organization, national or international, can be devised, which would enable just laws to be made and at the same time ensure that unjust laws were not made. The duty, then, of the citizen is on the one hand to help, as far as he can, in the construction of such political and economic institutions, in his own country and in the world, as will make it as easy as possible for the necessary knowledge on which just laws depend to be made available and for the law-makers to be disinterested in their desire for justice, and on the other hand to play his part in working the machinery as he ought.

We must now ask two final questions:—Which features in the political organization of the modern world make it likely, and which make it unlikely, that just laws will be made and just policies pursued? And what in general can be said about the way in which a man ought to think and act to-day in respect of his citizenship?

The assumption has above been made that if men thought and acted as they ought—that is, if their moral insight were disinterested and their knowledge of the relevant facts adequate—they would agree about the common purpose of humanity and the principles on which disagreements when they arose were to be determined. There are already certain services, such as the control of traffic, which (it can be said) every one is glad that the state should provide; and there are therefore some laws about the justice of which it can be supposed that general agreement has already been reached. It clearly does not follow that, simply because there is unanimity in some country about the state's provision of a particular service, it is *just* (that is, in the interest of humanity) that the service should be provided. But in fact services such as traffic control are of merely domestic importance, and it therefore happens not to matter, from the point of view of the world, that no consideration is given to other than national interests by the state that provides them.

Again, there are many activities (such as religion, music, art, literature, sport, and so on) in which men *can* engage without finding that their own interest and their neighbour's conflict. So it often happens

that, so far as certain departments of life are concerned, neither individuals nor nations find themselves in substantial disagreement; for it does not
necessarily follow (say) that the more enjoyment one
country obtains from music the less can its neighbour
obtain.

But many things which one individual or country
wants (a piece of territory, for instance) it cannot
have unless some other individual or country goes
without. When there is no agreement among the
members of the world-community either as to the
common purpose which ought to be followed or
the principles on which disputes ought to be decided,
under what conditions and by what process is it most
likely, considering the political organization of the
world to-day, that men will come to know and to do
what they ought?

If the discovery of justice is a creative act, requiring
a contribution from the experience of all those that
are concerned, it seems improbable that any one person or any one section of the community can hope to
know what justice demands in a given set of circumstances. It is most improbable of all when one party
to a dispute is the stronger, and can use its superior
strength to coerce the other. This is the position
when two nations of unequal power disagree (say,
China and Japan), and the rest of the world is not
prepared to interfere. It is also the position when one
section of a national community is able to make the
laws and decide the policy of the state, as in the

Dominion of South Africa, where the minority of white inhabitants have all the political power. Even when the franchise is extended to all the citizens of a state, it may happen that one section of the community is able to determine the policy and organization of a country, partly through political and partly through economic power, when conditions are such that the community is cut into various sections with sharply contrasted interests of their own. And even when such conditions do not prevail, the political parties may advocate programmes so widely divergent that the same result follows and the country is in fact governed by one party without any consideration for the other. When this happens, the parties are more properly described as factions, and the state is governed, as some city-states in Greece were at one time governed, by one faction after another, each in turn coming to power through some kind of revolutionary action. Finally, when a nation is responsible for the government of a subject people and is therefore the final arbiter of the laws and policy of that country, even if it has no financial or other material interest in the territory, it still has difficulty in discovering justice, partly because the very fact of its superior power tends to distort its judgement, and partly because it lacks that necessary knowledge of the facts which only the experience of the subjects can supply.

So it is suggested that where in fact the determination of policy is in the hands of one section of a community, whether the political organization of the place be called oligarchic, democratic, or dictatorial, there are grave dangers, amounting almost to certainty when the section represents a separate economic or cultural interest, that justice will not be done.

Must we conclude that these dangers can never be avoided so long as the world consists of nations some of which are stronger than others, and so long as within a nation there are groups of varying strength? In the absence of unanimity about the common purpose, is there no alternative to some form of dictatorship—to the imposition, that is, of one interpretation of justice upon those who have not contributed to the making of that interpretation? And is there no other reasonable hope at the present time than that within each nation the rival factions be equally matched, and that in the world as a whole a precarious peace be maintained by the balance of power?

If there is an alternative, it cannot be found, it would seem, by any individual who thinks that he personally (or his country, or any other group of which he is a member) can interpret justice correctly without the assistance of the other parties concerned. For, as we have seen, even if he (or his group) is not personally interested in the result of the decision, he has need of the experience of the people who are; and if he (or his group) *is* personally interested, not only does he need the experience of others, but he needs still more something that can help him to keep his moral judgement disinterested; further if he is not only interested, but also thinks that he can get what he wants without considering those who disagree with him, he is in an even worse position for acting as he ought. So it follows that the duty of any nation-state to-day is not to think (or to act as if it thought) that it is in a position to discern justice for itself, when disagreements arise with other states, but rather to recognize the limitations of its own experience and its own disinterestedness; in this sense, it must relinquish its claim to sovereignty. The same can be said of the duty of any section, party, or class within the nation, and of any individual too. Furthermore, each of these units has a positive duty to join in the creative activity of discovering justice, by contributing its own experience of the relevant facts, and its individual judgement of what ought to be done. For this to be possible, the world would have to be organized in such a way that the different experiences of people living in different parts of it could find adequate expression and be made generally available. Similarly, within each of these compartments of the world different experiences and different opinions would have to be used in the same kind of creative act.

But there is one condition that must be satisfied if justice is to be discovered in this fashion. The separate expressions of interest must be offered as contributions, on the understanding that no one of them claims to be that which ought finally to determine the laws and policy of the community without reference to the others. Only if this condition is fulfilled are the issues between the parties (whether within the state, or between states) likely to be such that a policy *can* eventually be found which is felt to be just by all concerned. If the condition is not fulfilled, a situation will arise out of which, in the absence of unanimity, dictatorship by one side or another is bound to follow, whether wearing the dress of legality or not, whether the dictatorship of a majority or of a minority, whether genuinely attempting to be disinterested or frankly selfish.

Generally speaking, this condition is more likely to be fulfilled when the only way in which force can be used is 'by due process of law', than when force is not confined to a single channel. The anarchy of the international situation is more certain to lead to injustice than the rule of law within a single state; and justice is less likely to be done in those social and economic parts of the national life which at the present time are affected indirectly or not at all by the law than in those parts into which the law has already directly entered in the name of social justice. But there can obviously be no certainty that under *all* circumstances the establishment of a political system will lead to better results than would have followed from the absence of any such system. It cannot, for instance, be said that the creation of a political organization to include all the nations of the world would by itself lead to the establishment of justice on earth; it could only do so if the stronger nations refused, for one

reason or another, to use the new political machinery
for the same purposes which now lead them to exploit
international anarchy. Further, it is obviously improbable that dictatorship will be avoided where
those who are the more powerful in economic and
other non-political respects, such as education, are
also politically the stronger; but it does not follow
that in an equalitarian society justice *will* be done, nor
ought we to conclude that except in an equalitarian society justice can *never* be done.

When this condition is in fact not fulfilled and the
only alternative to unanimity seems to be dictatorship (as at the present day in the world generally and
within most nations), how can the vicious circle be
broken? Must we wait for both sides in each dispute to do as they ought? No general answer can be
given to this question, but it seems probable that, until the stronger side in any dispute first voluntarily
makes a sacrifice, the dispute *cannot* be decided as it
ought to be. Even then justice will not be done, unless the other side follows the example of the stronger.
If it prefers to reap a sectional advantage by having
the dispute decided in its favour, the position of the
two parties in regard to strength will have been re-
versed, but the circle of injustice will remain un-
broken. However, what the effect on the world
would be if one group or one nation sacrificed itself
voluntarily (if, that is to say, when it had the power
to carry out its own interpretation of justice, it refused to do so, on the chance that its example might

be followed and an interpretation of justice be discovered through the mutual efforts of all parties to the dispute) no one can say; for not only can it be presumed that no such sacrifice has ever been made, but even if it had been made no one could ever know that the privileged position had been surrendered voluntarily.

What, finally, can be said about the duty of the citizen to-day? At each moment there is a unique set of circumstances in which each individual has to decide what his conscience bids him think and do. It would be as ridiculous to expect an answer to the particular question, which at any given moment a particular citizen is called on by the circumstances around him to answer, from any generalizations that can be made about citizenship, as it would be (if we may borrow an analogy from Bacon) to try to find the way from London to York by studying Ortelius' map of the universe. How ought I to vote in the next election? What steps can I take to prevent another war? Is it my duty to take revolutionary action against the present government? These, and innumerable other questions of the same kind, may have to be asked and answered by the individual citizen from time to time, and it would be vain to attempt an answer to them in general terms. But is there nothing to be said, except that the citizen must do the best he can as each concrete problem presents itself? Not much, perhaps, but this at least:—

First, the citizen must be realistic. The more he

reflects on his own life and on the state of affairs in the world of which he is a part, the more he ought to be impressed at the greatness of the gulf which seems fixed between what is and what ought to be. Secondly, he may reflect that the political organization of his own and other countries is simply one part of a complex everchanging environment which has always surrounded him and will always surround him. His citizenship is one aspect of his manhood, and though for the purposes of thought and discussion he must make abstractions and talk of personal, social, economic, or political problems, reality is not divided into separate compartments, and his thinking can never compass truth unless he remembers that this is so. If there are ethical problems at all, then ethical problems must arise from the fact of his citizenship, just as certainly as they arise from his relationship with his friends or any other part of his environment. Thirdly, if he knows that he has a duty in his private life which he constantly fails either to recognize correctly or to fulfil, he must not be surprised when his honest attempt to examine realistically the political facts of the modern world, and compare them with what he feels that they ought to be, reveals a situation that he has to recognize as desperately discouraging.

But if, in the fourth place, he refuses to be fatalistic about his own life, believing rather that his will is capable of freedom and need not necessarily be determined by his environment, then he must also believe that it is possible, in the fullness of time and after centuries of effort, that men, even in their corporate capacity as members of different groups, will free themselves of the sin that so easily besets them and succeed in loving one another. He may reflect, on the other hand, that man finds his life only when he is prepared to lose it, and that in actual experience no one can love his neighbour without sacrificing himself, in greater or less degree; and the conclusion seems to follow that only when the spirit of self-sacrifice, which men learn from their personal friendships, has so infected the groups to which they belong that those groups are prepared to sacrifice themselves for each other's good, will justice be done on earth.

Lastly, when he considers the immediate problem of what he ought to do next, and finds that whether he likes it or not he is a member of a nation-state, he may do well to notice that the state is one of the means through which he is enabled to hate or love certain of his neighbours. Those of his neighbours who are also, by the accident of birth or residence, his fellow countrymen, have a special claim on him; for since they speak his language, and in other ways share with him a particular cultural inheritance, they alone are able to co-operate with him in the realization of a particular form of the good life; and of this purpose the state is potentially one of the necessary instruments. Towards those of his neighbours who happen to be of some other nationality, his duty is much harder to perform; for his personal relationship to them is in fact more remote; the difficulty of behaving to them as he ought, or even of discovering how he ought to behave, is proportionately more serious; and in this part of his duty he must at present expect the state to be rather a hindrance than a help.

As part, then, of his duty to his neighbour he will find that he has two kinds of political duty, that of helping to make the policy and laws of the state what they ought to be, and that of obeying the law (except when he feels that he must disobey it in order to carry out the first aspect of his duty) in such a way that the evil effects, which are liable to attend even just laws, do not follow. The choice of a particular procedure by which to attempt the first of these duties depends naturally on a multitude of circumstances and especially on the civic rights which the state allows him: whether (for instance) he has the vote, what measure of free speech he is allowed, and so on. It may be his duty to take no immediate steps towards altering the law; it may be his duty to proceed by the means which the existing law provides; and it may be his duty to use methods which the existing law does not allow. But how far he succeeds in doing his duty (whatever his procedure may be) will depend ultimately on the strength or weakness of his *disinterestedness*—that is, of his desire to see justice done without regard for his personal convenience—and on the extent or limitation of his *knowledge*; the former will be conditioned, in turn, by the success or failure of his efforts to recognize and deliver himself from the prejudices with which his environment and education

have endowed him; and the latter by his personal experience and by his powers of sympathy and understanding. He may fight or refuse to fight; he may go
to gaol, or receive the highest honours from a grate-
ful nation; and it is by these signs that the world, following the lead of one or other of the many schools of
sentimentality—war-mongers, peace-mongers, and
the rest—will judge him.

A man may be called a patriot by his imperialist
friends or his pacifist enemies, though in truth it
might more properly be said of him:

> His desire is a dureless content,
>   And a trustless joy;
>   He is won with a world of despair,
>   And is lost with a toy.

But when such a man is said to love his country, and
to be a patriot, it is another instance of

> the word love abused,
> Under which many childish desires
> And conceits are excused.

And in fact, I suggest, it is only such a quality as
wise disinterestedness that distinguishes the man who
truly loves his country from the traitor; and only the
man who truly loves his country can properly be
called a patriot.

> But true love is a durable fire,
>   In the mind ever burning,
> Never sick, never dead, never cold,
>   From itself never turning.

And the true love of the patriot for his country is of such a kind that the more he loves his own country the more capable he finds himself of loving other countries as he loves his own.

IV. SOCIAL INEQUALITIES

By C. R. MORRIS

OUR task is to consider social inequalities as presenting a problem of personal ethics. Let us first attempt to review the facts.

Actually, the facts about social classes are not easy to determine. The structure of modern society is a highly complicated one, and the attempt to analyse it by the well-regulated engines of accurate observation and disciplined inference from statistics, essential to the credit of modern science, is still in its infancy. It is therefore possible for publicists in this field to make from time to time statements of whose falsity we may be morally certain, but which we cannot finally refute by appeal to accepted evidence. Bearing these difficulties in mind, however, we must do the best we can.

It is difficult to say of what we are conscious when we are class-conscious. The most obvious constituent element which leaps to the mind is a fellow-feeling for people of the same kind, together with a recognition that that kind has its place in a more or less definite hierarchy of kinds—that is, it has some kinds above it and some kinds below it. In ordinary language class-consciousness connotes a definite sense in the class-conscious person of superiority of some kind to the classes beneath, and of inferiority of some kind to the classes above. It does not ordinarily connote any real pride of class; for though no doubt many middle-class persons, who are highly class-conscious, are genuinely convinced that the upper middle class are the salt of the earth, and genuinely despise the 'damned aristocrat', there are far more class-conscious people who are proud indeed of not belonging to a lower class, but who would be prouder of belonging to a higher one.

What, then, are these social classes? There is, of course, a famous view abroad—a view which seems to be treated to-day with ever-increasing respect by many writers and thinkers who will never agree with it—which gives a simple answer to this question. Class distinctions, it says, depend upon property. The fundamental rift in human society is between those who have property and those who have not. It is not, it is to be remarked, basically and fundamentally between those who have a larger yearly income to spend and those who have a smaller one. It is between those who own property and those who do not. It may seem to some that for all practical purposes this is a distinction without a difference. But from the point of view of understanding or misunderstanding the Marxist theory it is of great importance.

The basic distinction, on this view, is the distinction between the capitalist and the proletarian, the man with property and the man with nothing but his labour. The man who lives by selling his labour and skill for wages, even if his wages are large enough, and secure enough, to be called a salary, is as such a proletarian. It is true that if his wages and circumstances allow he may, by saving his wages, become an owner of property; he will then to a greater or less extent lose his status as a proletarian, and also the mental attitude of a proletarian, without wholly taking on the status and attitude of the capitalist; he will thus help to form an intermediate class. But the important classes are the pure proletariat and the pure capitalists. It is between these that the vital struggle lies. There may, indeed, be far more actual bitterness of feeling between the proletarians and the middle class. For the latter, being able to maintain themselves at a higher standard of living than would fall to their lot in an equalitarian state, are staunch supporters of the *status quo*, and, politically, are the strongest pillar of support which the capitalist system has, seeing that they are far more numerous than the pure capitalists. But to the proletarian the man of the middle class is not himself the real enemy, though he may appear as such because the real enemy cannot be reached except over his dead body.

This view of the essential nature of the division between classes, as was said earlier on, is a simple one. Equally simple is the explanation which its votaries offer of the inevitable course of future history. The community, it says, will become more and more sharply divided into capitalist and proletarian; the middle class will go either up or down. Capitalists become purer and purer capitalists, and fewer and fewer in number; the rest become purely proletarian.

The community thus approaches nearer and nearer to an unmediated, face-to-face opposition of a few pure capitalists to a multitude of wage-slaves. Then at last the truth about the structure of society is obvious to the meanest intelligence. Inevitably the proletarians remove the capitalists, and destroy the capitalistic system. There follows necessarily a period when the community is controlled by people of proletarian mentality in the interests of proletarians. For this period, which in accordance with the demands of the Marxian dialectic must be regarded as the antithesis of the preceding capitalistic society, there is little to be said except that it is superior to capitalism, and that it offers hope in so far as it carries within its womb the seed of the future community—the classless society of true communism, in which there is neither bond nor free, Jew nor Gentile, capitalist nor proletarian.

Now this whole view, like most studies in dialectic, strikes the ordinary observer as too neat and simple, both as a reading of the structure of existing society and as a reading of future history. If we consider the theory in its fully rounded form, as I have tried to give it, the most striking things about it, from the point of view which concerns us here, are, I think, its extremely formal and pessimistic interpretation of the present and its extremely formal and optimistic view of the future. As regards the future it is utopian in its belief in the perfectionism of human nature. Out of an entirely unregenerate present as thesis, and an only less unregenerate antithesis—for the proletarian acquired his essential character under the iniquitous régime of the capitalist, the thesis to his antithesis— there is to emerge by the synthesis of opposites the perfection of human nature and the millennium of the classless society. I do not say that this utopian optimism is entirely without support from experience, even though it may be the fact that, in some of its votaries at least, it rests mainly on a touching faith in dialectic. It is likely that a period of supremacy of the proletariat, if it could occur, would change the character of the proletarian, so that a new order would supervene. Many will think that it could only be a better order; but few would expect it to be the Marxian millennium.

But even if we allow that this interpretation of society is too formal, and that the results of its analysis are too neat and simple, at least it may serve to give us a lead in our attempt to determine the true nature of social classes in society as we know it. And perhaps it is well to remind ourselves here of the wisdom of Plato. It was his view, as expressed in the *Republic*, that as soon as the community fails to be the Ideal State, it automatically finds itself on the road to becoming two communities instead of one—a community of the rich set over against a community of the poor—and its future history is determined by the inevitable struggle between these two. The state may be ruled by the rich, ruling as such, or by the poor, ruling as such, or, worst of all, by a tyrant—a depraved form of government whose establishment is possible only when the citizens have become degenerate by living under these bad régimes. But in any case the condition of society is evil, and there is no real health or happiness in it. Plato allows, indeed, of an intermediate condition, which he calls timocracy, between the best and the beginning of the worst; but, broadly speaking, his warning is that under everything but the ideally best constitution the struggle between rich and poor is inevitable and is the primary factor in determining the life of the state. In the ideal constitution itself, of course, everything is otherwise. Here the best people are not rich, and do not wish to be rich, because in such a society the ends of life can be secured without riches, and the best people are too intelligent to think that wealth was ever anything but a means. Under this constitution, if any one wishes to pile up riches he is allowed to do so, very much as under almost any constitution people who wish to are allowed to play harmless games. But the whole tone of life is set by the best people, who are not concerned with riches, but with the things that really matter.

On the main point the Marxist theory, which we were examining just now, agrees. It does not maintain that it is the last word about human nature that man is the economic man. Indeed, its whole teaching is to the contrary. In the present state of things man is the economic man. But that is the fault, according to the theory, not of human nature, but of the present system of society. In the fullness of time we shall come to the fine flowering of human freedom in a classless society, in which the struggle for economic gain will have disappeared. As in Plato and all the greatest thinkers, there is nothing the matter with human nature itself; only it is an inexorable law that man can only come to his full goodness in so far as the society in which he lives allows him to do so. When his condition allows him to grow to his full stature, man is a god.

It is now high time that we turned to our own analysis of the nature of social classes; though we may reasonably hope, I think, that this examination of a famous view may have helped to clear our minds. At least it has reminded us that there is little essential difference of opinion among all the great thinkers in regard to the ultimate moral destiny of man. And this may help us to keep a sense of proportion.

In society as we know it the Marxist theory of classes is not confirmed by the facts. The middle class, which has neither the outlook of the pure capitalist nor that of the pure proletarian, seems to be in no danger of disappearing. The middle-class man is a very real permanent, making for social stability, and indeed almost for social immobility, with a quiet effectiveness that has surprised most of us since the war, and continues to surprise us. Moreover, the man of the middle class does not seem to be merely oscillating between the mentality of the capitalist and the mentality of the proletarian. He has a very positive and definite attitude and scale of values of his own, which seems to be lasting and to be the most powerful force determining the tone of life of the community as a whole. Not only does the middle-class man exist in larger numbers than the man with the pure capitalist outlook or the man with the pure proletarian outlook; but he remains permanently fixed in his own attitude of mind, and shows little desire to change in the one direction or the other. He is neither merely exploited like the proletarian, nor merely exploiting like the capitalist. He depends for his living mainly on working for a wage, but he is not so utterly without substance, and without stable position in the community, that he either is, or feels, a mere wage-slave, or even predominantly a wage-slave. He is neither in utter control of himself and his economic destiny, nor entirely a pawn in the control of others or of the system. He stands somewhere in the middle, and he can have a certain modicum of self-respect. He feels neither a superman, as the pure capitalist is conceived to be, nor a slave, like the pure proletarian.

There seem to be no effective forces at work in English society to-day to drive this middle class out of existence. Whatever surprises the future may hold, it is certain that the development of the social structure of Great Britain in the coming generations will be profoundly influenced by the scale of values of the British middle class. It is only necessary to look at the Trade Union movement with the eye of a proletarian to be convinced of that.

This does not mean that there are not also a large number of people whose position and life is very near to those of the pure proletarian, as the Marxist conceives him. Moreover, under the economic conditions of the past ten years, a large number of these have been, and are, people who have the skill, general ability, and character to make a contribution well above that of the average man to the wealth and welfare of the community. This condition of affairs, in which a large section of people of skill and energy have nothing to do, presents perhaps the gravest social and political problem of our time. It is a condition which must sooner or later shake the foundations of any social system which fails to remove it. But we must let that pass for the moment; for here it concerns us only as one of the facts which we must consider.

Enough, then, has been said to show that the Marxist theory of classes on the face of it does not come very near to giving a satisfactory explanation of the division of society into classes in Great Britain as we find it to-day. It seems to throw little or no light on the obvious class divisions which we see around us. It simply does not seem to be talking about our problem, the problem of *social* classes, at all. Of course the Marxist will maintain that the obvious class divisions do not matter, being of no real importance; and that what does matter is the more fundamental division of which he is speaking—a division which is not obvious but hidden, and does not correspond to the obvious social divisions. But, be that as it may, let us now look at these obvious social divisions.

So far we have been speaking of social classes as if they were an economic phenomenon, based entirely on economic considerations, and being divisions that arise among purely economic men. But it is a question whether to do this is not to miss the main force of our special problem. It is doubtful whether among a society of purely economic men the phenomenon of social classes, as we know them, would ever arise at all. We are not here primarily concerned with the problem that arises in a community just because one set of people have motor-cars and another set of people want them and cannot have them. No doubt this situation gives rise to genuine difficulties. But it does not in itself present a specifically *social* problem, though a social problem may quite well gather round it. If it happens that those who have motor-cars experience a great fellow-feeling for one another, which drives them together into a compact group, with a strong feeling of internal solidarity as against all people who have not motor-cars; and if similarly those who have not motor-cars are bound together with a similar feeling of solidarity as against those who have motor-cars—then the problem of social classes has arisen. This problem will no doubt tend very strongly to grow up around an economic division; but it need not necessarily do so, and it does not always do so. The feeling of solidarity between genuine artists may very well prove a stronger tie than the solidarity of the prosperous and the solidarity of the penurious; similarly the solidarity of educated men may prove more binding than the division of rich and poor. And it is certainly the case that the solidarity of blue blood has sometimes stood firm for more than a generation against the pull of acute economic division.

Specifically social division, then, tends to gather round economic division, but it is not the same thing and it does not always do so. We are concerned here with social division, and not with economic division, except in so far as the discussion of the latter is necessary for dealing with the former.

Broadly speaking, we may say that in a society where the one thing that matters to everybody is to have a motor-car, a strong social solidarity will be likely to arise between those people who have no motor-car. But in a society where the one thing that mattered to people was to be educated, and where all education was conducted on a scholarship system (so that nobody could buy an education), there would be no feeling of solidarity between people who did not own motor-cars, but there would be likely to grow up a strong solidarity between people who could not pass examinations—and the more so in proportion as it was recognized that educated persons enjoy admittedly real benefits which are denied to the uneducated. A society can quite well be imagined in which there would be an aggressive social solidarity between people who loved music; and some have dreamed of a community in which the solidarity of all Oxford men would stand triumphantly against all other influence. All those who have any experience of the life of large schools, or of universities, know well how there can arise within a society very strong social divisions, which may cause great bitterness and pain, but which are not based on economic considerations, nor do they run parallel to social divisions in the larger communities of town, county, or nation.

When we bear all this in mind, we see at once that it is not easy to imagine a classless society. Men are obviously different from one another; they have different interests and different capacities. It seems inconceivable that they should not group themselves according to those interests and capacities, and that the solidarity of some of the groups should not become very strong. It seems certain too that this solidarity will normally be strongest in those groups which are distinguished on a basis of capacity in regard to the major interests of the community at large. It is difficult to see how this could be avoided. If the most aggressive social divisions are those based on the primary interests of members of the society, it cannot fail to happen that some of the groups will be more powerful, and will receive greater respect, within the community than others. For instance, in a society which cared most for learning, the most learned people would certainly tend to group together, and would receive a great measure of respect and standing. If that is so, there is bound to be genuine class dominance up to a point, and genuine class feeling.

Two questions then arise: Do social inequalities in themselves do great harm? Or is it only when social inequalities are based on economic considerations that they have a vitally prejudicial effect?

Let us consider the second point first. It will not be disputed that when social divisions exactly coincide with serious economic divisions they do enormous harm to the social life of a community. By economic divisions here is meant not differences of economic occupation but differences of wealth. As has been said before, the difficulties which arise from the fact that some people have this world's goods while others have not is in itself a different difficulty from that which arises from the hostility of social classes. It may in the end cause greater offence to social stability and peace, or it may cause less; but the two things are not the same thing. But when both go together, then the cleavage in society is serious indeed. It is bad enough when one class of persons is exclusive of, and hostile to, another class of persons, so that each class stands together solid within itself and is apt to find itself opposed to the other on important community issues—witness the bitter hostility which has sometimes arisen between a rich merchant class and an aristocracy, which was not relevantly richer or poorer. But when one of the classes in question is on the whole well endowed with this world's goods and the other is on the whole poor, then there

is an immense surcharge of bitterness in the class hostility. We all know this well from experience. It may
not be the case—as we have seen, it is not by any means
wholly the case—that class differences in Great Britain
to-day depend on differences of wealth. But the fact
remains that they correspond very roughly to broad
economic differences, and this very noticeable fact
tends to produce extremely shrill overtones of bitter
animosity.

A great deal is gained, then, if it can be brought
about that social differences do not depend, and *obviously* do not depend, on economic differences. Most
people, I suppose, from what may be called the
middle-middle classes upwards would say that they
do not so depend. Certainly all those who have access
to the higher education system of this country know
well that there are several cross-influences of great
power, which prevent mere economic distinctions
from wholly determining class divisions. But for
those below the middle-middle classes the case is different. To them the main divisions seem too exactly
to correspond to the possession or non-possession of
this world's goods. They know little or nothing of
the class-feeling between the middle-middle classes
and the upper-middle classes, or between the boys
and girls of the municipal secondary schools and
those of the public school class. What is most obvious to them, and what is most obvious to any one
who knows something of their problems, is the fairly
compact solidarity of those who can attain to more

than a certain material standard of living as against those who cannot. We must be careful not to exaggerate this. But, broadly speaking, it is true to say that to the upper and middle classes class distinctions appear to depend only partly on considerations of wealth or standard of living, while to the lower classes they appear to depend almost entirely on these things. And, as has been said before, where class distinctions are associated with economic differences, there is an immense surcharge of bitterness. This is a grave problem.

The question is, Can anything be done in the matter? If what was said previously is sound, then in a community in which wealth is regarded as of very great importance there are in the end only two alternatives: *either* we must learn to put up with this degree of class war, mitigating it as far as possible by minimizing the obstacles to migration between classes; *or* economic differences must be abolished, if that is possible. On the other hand, in a community, if such can be imagined, in which wealth was regarded as of very little importance, this particular trouble would hardly arise. Nobody would notice that social differences roughly corresponded to economic differences, and nobody would mind if he did notice. Nor is this condition of affairs, as a matter of fact, entirely remote from all experience. To take only one instance, there is many a man of scholarly tastes, who, if he noticed that the very rich only invited one another to their tables and never invited him or his like, would (being sufficiently comfortably off himself) merely smile. As Aristotle would say with his great common sense, the wise man, armed with his knowledge that wealth is not of great importance, *plus* a competence of this world's goods for himself, can live the good life untroubled by considerations of wealth.

Now it is quite true that, as compared with the things that really matter, wealth does not matter. As compared with the things that really give pleasure, wealth does not give pleasure, and cannot substantially contribute to pleasure. Everybody knows that the great philosophers and seers of all ages have taught this. Everybody knows that the New Testament teaches this, and goes out of its way to emphasize the point again and again. Everybody knows that it is true. The kingdom of heaven is within us. We all know that when we are most deeply admonishing ourselves or others about the deepest things we must, regardless of all circumstances, teach with the great teachers that the mind must be its own place, and that the good man must rise above the slings and arrows of outrageous fortune. There is no other way to peace or happiness. The theoretic communist recognizes this as well as any one else. It is only in a bad society, he says, when man is not truly himself, that wealth is the supreme thing that matters. But, he adds, all experience goes to show that, so long as there are differences of wealth, wealth will remain the thing that matters. It is only in a society where every one has equal access to this world's goods that wealth will take its proper place in the scale of values, and man will concentrate his attention on the things that really satisfy.

Now we must take it, I suppose, that the great majority of the people of this country are more or less committed against this equalitarian view, even as an ideal. If that is so, and if what we have previously argued is sound, then some other way than the communist's way must be found of producing a community in which wealth is not over-valued. This is no doubt not impossible. But it is certainly not easy. It is perhaps the most difficult thing in the world for the rich man to convince the poor man, and especially the very poor man, that he really means what he says when he says that wealth is of little or no importance. We shall never have a society in which differences of wealth are powerless to contribute bitterness to social distinctions until everybody really in his heart and mind, and in his actions too, entirely *believes* that wealth is of little or no importance. And in this it is obvious that those who are most respected must lead the way. So long as any class in the community puts its own rights as regards wealth above all other considerations, so long will wealth have this terrible power to cleave society. Let it be said, in justice to the possibilities of even our existing social system, that the man who shows that he is largely above considerations of wealth is admired by and is acceptable to all classes of the community. But very few men are capable of giving this impression of themselves. Of very few men, of course, is it *true* that they are unaffected by considerations of wealth. But even where it was true, it would still be very difficult indeed for the rich man to convince the poor man that he means what he says in this matter. It has never really been demonstrated that there is more than the one way to do it.

We have said enough of the problem caused by the coincidence of social and economic distinctions. Let us now examine that which arises from social distinctions alone in their awful purity; that is to say, roughly speaking, the problem of social classes as it appears to persons of the middle-middle classes and upwards.

When all is said, it must be admitted that class distinctions, even when they do not coincide with differences of wealth, are an ugly phenomenon and have effects which are very serious for the community. The tendency, where it exists, for a man to live confined within any class or group is nothing short of a social disaster. The knowledge of such a man will be limited, and his capacity to understand far more limited still. He will find it more and more difficult as time goes on to recognize in any one who does not show the main characteristics to which he is accustomed the character of a human being at all. If he is a good man, he will call his rational self to his aid, and will say to himself—I must remember that even this man is one of God's creatures. But it is hardly an exaggeration to say that this does more harm than good. It requires a saint or a god to offer effective sympathy to one whom he does not in the least understand. It has often been said that the public schoolboy can have no fellow-feeling for any one who does not believe that the rules of cricket hold in every department of life, though nobody else in the world but the public schoolboy does believe this. It has often been said that the Englishman cannot understand any one who does not subscribe to the proposition that every man and woman in the world wants, or ought to want, to be an English gentleman. These statements, perhaps, are caricatures; perhaps, too, they are out of date. But every one knows that a fundamental problem lies here —a problem which cannot be written off at a stroke by a good resolution overnight. It is a problem which goes to the root of education, and especially of self-education.

It is clear that it is a problem which will last. Men are very different from one another, and will always be so. Any one who has had a fair opportunity to enjoy reasonable social intercourse knows that he will always be happiest in a world which it takes all sorts to make. And so long as men are different they will always associate themselves into groups or classes. And some of the groups or classes will always be more respected, and have more standing and influence of one kind and another in the community at large. And some men, and some groups of men, will always wish to be included within other groups, which will not or cannot have them. And this will create some feeling.

This will always be so; it cannot but be so. But need there be so much animosity? Need there be real and serious disharmony within society? Need it be made so difficult for us not to notice differences of type, that we are unable to go to meet people spontaneously, not as types, but as real persons?

On the whole, the overwhelming verdict of educated men is that in an educated society such disharmony is not unavoidable. It is often claimed that it is the great triumph of the British public schools that they succeed in making all sorts of people, with all sorts of backgrounds, capable of getting on well together, recognizing differences between one another, but without serious envy or bitter feeling of any kind. It is also said that our great universities are pre-eminently successful in accomplishing the same thing on an even wider scale. And though this claim is sometimes over-stated, and though it is also commonly said that this result, where it is achieved, is achieved at the too great cost of pressing every one into the same mould; yet broadly speaking we may allow that the claim is substantially justified. The public schools and universities of this country do help the young to learn in their bones that it takes several sorts to make a world, and that those several sorts, even if people of each sort tend to group themselves closely together for their greater edification and comfort, can yet live together in a wider society without social disharmony, and even with some measure of lively unity.

The irony of the situation is that the great majority of the nation, and nearly all foreign observers, look upon the public schools and ancient universities as the main influence operating to maintain the extraordinary persistence and stability of class distinctions in this country. The fact is that their success in producing a high degree of social solidarity within the pale is in practice correlated with a high degree of exclusiveness of all persons outside the pale, however unintentional such exclusiveness may be. Understanding and fellow-feeling within the classes that are solid seem to go with the erection of an apparently impregnable rampart against all others. This rampart is quite impassable by other groups or classes, and can usually be surmounted by individuals only at the cost of pretence—the pretence of being really at home within the charmed circle. The appearances to those outside certainly are that any one within the pale can converse with any one outside only as one within conversing with one who is without, and not as two individuals might who met one another unencumbered by any social affiliations. Further, the appearances to those outside are that the individual, even with the best intentions in the world and with a considerable degree of self-command, cannot of himself effectively lower this barrier. So much harm has already been done that it is almost impossible, except under the most favourable and unusual circumstances, for two persons who are members of different social classes to meet really as man to man. Those people who have the most experience of coming into contact with all sorts of men and women are in general most keenly aware of the existence of this difficulty. While their experience may make the actual difficulty less, it commonly makes their sensitivity to it greater. And everybody is aware of its ill effects both in regard to the full life of the individual and as concerns social harmony.

Now if it is true, as I think it is true, that British education has in a large measure this priceless secret of welding all kinds of people into a social whole, making them such that with all their differences they can live together in unity, it is surely profoundly sad, and also profoundly silly, that we should allow our system of national education to be the main influence which serves efficiently to perpetuate the most persistent and stable class system in the western world. It may be true, no doubt it is true, that class hostility is not as bitter in this country as it has been from time to time in other countries. Let us be thankful for that. But its effects are bad enough, as everybody knows; and the deadening permanence and emotional impenetrability of the barriers between social classes is perhaps the most powerful cause preventing an effective, united effort in solving national difficulties. Yet it is almost certain that it is within our power to abolish the worst effects of class hostility by so overhauling our national system of education as to make full use of that mysterious power, ingrained in the British tradition of education, to make *all* sorts live together in real unity. We have surely come to the time when it is clear that a powerful machine like the public school system, so long as it is used to create lasting social solidarity on an improperly narrow basis, does more harm than good. If this is so, it is a criminal waste of one of the most priceless gifts which has ever been handed down from the past to any generation.

In conclusion, then, does the existence of social inequalities present a problem of personal ethics? It is quite clear that it does. The necessary changes in society are of such a kind that they cannot come until the community is ready for them, and cannot in the end be permanently effected except by the quiet influence of the living and talking of individuals. It is certain that in the good society every man must live up to the knowledge that the possession of wealth is not the supreme end of man. It is also certain that in the good society education both in the school and in the home must be such as to produce real social harmony in the whole community from end to end. It must be allowed that, as things are, we can none of us, as individuals, really live, or effectively encourage one another to live, as if we knew these things to be true without the severest struggle with ourselves. Yet it is only in proportion as more and more individuals succeed in doing this that the good society can come into being.

In this country we pride ourselves on our mainten-

ance of free institutions and of personal liberty. We
have so far refused to use our political machinery to
force ourselves and one another, as individuals, in
these matters. We have declined to attempt to change
the attitude of the community to wealth by making it
impossible by legislation for any one to have wealth.
We have declined to force ourselves to find out the
advantages of a different system of education by driving all children by legislation into the same schools.
We tend to forget that this is reasonable only if the individual accepts his proper responsibility. The good
man has an unanswerable case against being forced to
do what somebody else thinks to be right, because he
does spontaneously and with energy what he thinks
to be right himself. The man who never concerns
himself at all with what is right has no such case. Only
so long as the individual is actively good, or at least
so long as a fair proportion of individuals are actively
good, can the way of free institutions and personal
liberty justify itself as a means of eradicating real and
recognized social evils.

V. EARNING AND SPENDING

By R. L. HALL

ETHICS is primarily concerned with our relations with others; 'earning and spending' are concerned with material wealth—whatever can be bought and sold. We have therefore to consider in this lecture the effect on others of our economic activities. The subject is a controversial one, and to treat it shortly will require rather dogmatic methods.

Although it is a truism that material wealth does not in itself bring happiness, it is difficult to convince either ourselves or others of its truth. This is because the possibility of happiness depends so much upon the possession of wealth: it is almost impossible to attain any of the ends men set before themselves if we are constantly under-fed, cold, or unhealthy. Overwork, unless arising out of interest in the work itself, and uncertainty about the material future are also barriers shutting us off from the things we want to do. We cannot say any more than this, but it is common experience that wealth enables us to avoid the more obvious pains and discomforts and gives us the possibility of a satisfactory life; though whether we avail ourselves of this or not depends on other circumstances. We can begin, therefore, with the assumption that it is to the common interest to solve the economic problem, that of the scarcity of material wealth.

P

Our wants are greater than our means of satisfying them, and everything we make needs time and material with which we might have made something else. Every community has to decide what sort of goods to produce, in what quantities and by what methods to make them, and in what way they shall be shared when they have been made; the arrangements by which these things are done comprise the economic system. And though no economic system has ever been one of completely free competition, in most modern countries it is still to a predominant extent controlled by the choice of individuals. The combined effect of individual actions, that is, determines the material condition of the community, so that it is necessary for the individual to understand the effect of what he does; and even when he is unimportant he should remember that most of us are in the same position, and that the sum of our actions may be decisive.

The system is still essentially that described by the economists of *laisser faire*, though it has been modified by the activities of state and private organizations. If a man sets himself to earn as much as possible from his labour or his property, he will naturally choose the occupation which offers him the highest yield. This will cause goods and services to be made in such quantities that the products of similar efforts will exchange for one another. For if one occupation is more profitable than another, those who are able to do so will leave the less and enter the more remunerative, thus altering the quantities made and therefore the prices at which the goods will sell, which depend ultimately on the supply available. And if people are prepared to pay just those prices which represent the difficulty of producing each separate article, these articles must be satisfying the wants of the community more fully than they would at other prices.

In short, it pays to make what the community wants, and it is obvious that it pays to use the most efficient of the processes available: and competition, if it were unimpeded, would tend to produce this result. Though competition is not free, owing to state regulations and to ignorance of profitable openings or inability to take advantage of them, yet in most cases some approximation to freedom is reached; and where this is so the greater the disparity between prices and cost of production, the less likely is it that it will continue.

It follows from this that the man who is making the most profitable use of his energies or his property is acting not only wisely but well, in his own interest and in that of society. The fact that an occupation is profitable shows that its products are wanted, and as between two wants it is better to supply the more urgent. Since the available labour and capital are scarce, they should be used in the best way, and this is likely to be the way for which most is offered. We shall have to consider later the modifications which must be made in this statement, but there is a strong *prima facie* argument that the successful man is helping others as well as himself, while the unsuccessful is wasting the limited resources of the community. It can be laid down as a general rule, in fact, that if a man is earning a satisfactory income he is also contributing to the welfare of his fellows; whilst if he is not earning anything, he must be living on the efforts of others.

This must not be taken as a condemnation of the unemployed, who constitute such an urgent social problem in many countries at present. Most of these are people anxious to find some occupation, and their position is due to circumstances over which they have little control. Yet in all classes of society there are those who take advantage of arrangements for the distressed in order to live without contributing anything, and it would be a disservice to the real unemployed not to point out that life would be impossible for us all if such an attitude were a general one.

What is the position of those who have all the income they require from the possession of property? The property is producing wealth; but there is a sense in which it can be argued that they are themselves a burden on the community. The question is a difficult one, and we must content ourselves with a brief statement of the arguments for and against private ownership. The strongest objection seems to be that inherited wealth is distributed in a haphazard manner which offends our sense of equity, since it depends on the accident of parentage. It is also

argued that the possession of property enables its
owners to accumulate more, and thus large differences
of wealth arise which are themselves a source of unhappiness owing to our unfortunate propensity to
want what others have. Further, if the whole income
were spread more evenly among the community,
some of the urgent needs of the poor would be met
from what is superfluity to the rich. And since there
are few occupations which can be carried on without
capital, the owners of it are in a position to affect the
lives of their fellows very deeply if they are incom-
petent or capricious.

The strongest argument in favour of property is
that on the whole an economic society organized on
this basis is a practical one, which does succeed in
supporting most of its members; while communal
ownership does not work at all easily in a complex
modern state, because it has no mechanism which
automatically corrects inefficiency as losses do under
competition. It is not inevitable that a communal state
must collapse; but unless it is conducted with great
skill and determination there is some presumption
that we might all be worse off under it.

It is hard to form an opinion which is not affected
by our own wealth or lack of it. Until there has been
a revolutionary change there is nothing to be gained
by giving away what we have, since it would pre-
sumably come into other private hands. But there is
a serious responsibility on those who have great possessions; and it is in the general interest that these

should be used in the most efficient way, which (subject to reservations shortly to be made) is also the most profitable one. If the owner of property feels that he should do something, it is probable, as in the case of the wage-earner, that he will be of most service if he does what is best paid; though, as we shall see later, he has special opportunities of making contributions to the common welfare of a kind the value of which cannot be measured by money.

So far, then, we have reached the conclusion that if we earn as much as we can we are doing our best to reduce that scarcity of material wealth which is the cause of all economic activity. We must now consider exceptions to this general rule—methods of earning which are not advantageous to others; and to do this it is necessary to understand the conception of a fair exchange, which has often exercised the ingenuity of philosophers. In an ordinary exchange each person wants what he gets more than what he gives away— when I buy a hat I want it more than the money; but the hatter prefers what I pay him, so that we have each gained from the transaction. Thus there is some meaning in saying that an exchange is fair when each party to it is getting what he thinks he is. If this is so, then even if what he gets is worthless in the eyes of others, it must be satisfactory to him or he would not have made the transaction. The case in which he is forced to do so will be considered later, when we are dealing with monopolies.

Now if an exchange is not a fair one in this sense,

the income received by the person who gains from
it does not involve an equivalent contribution to the
common stock. The simplest example of this is steal-
ing, where there is no return whatever. And further,
if the parties to exchanges have to be always on their
guard against deception, valuable effort is wasted on
precautions of the nature of police measures. To be
a cause of expenditure which would not otherwise
have been required is to make a negative contribution
to society, as in the familiar example of the glazier who
employed men to break windows so that he could
mend them.

Thus all kinds of misrepresentation, even when
they are allowed by the deficiencies or practical difficulties of the law, are on a different footing from
ordinary transactions. The practice is least objectionable when both sides engage in it, being then of the
nature of gambling: in which (though we may object
to it on other grounds) there is at least a satisfaction
from the transaction itself. The deceptions which
take place in dealings in horses and in second-hand
goods of all kinds, when they are confined to dealers,
are almost a recognized rule of what may be considered an amusement in itself; a community cannot live by gambling or swindling alone, for if it tried
to do so, it would produce nothing with which to
gamble or swindle. But when members of the public
are involved the case is different, since they have no
time to become expert, and usually get little direct
satisfaction from deals in which on the average they

must lose. It may be pleasant enough to buy some valuable object for a small sum through the ignorance of the owner (if, that is to say, we can forget the ethical aspect of the matter); but it cannot be questioned that for the community as a whole the dissatisfactions outweigh the satisfactions.

Many examples of exchanges which are unfair because of ignorance can be found all through the economic world. The opportunities for making money by the flotation of companies which are not likely to justify the optimistic statements of their prospectuses are well known: all those engaged in such businesses are adding little to our wealth. In the same way, certain kinds of advertising, which appeal to the hopes or fears of the public in matters about which they must be ignorant, are closely akin to direct misrepresentation, since they cause people to spend their money under the influence of quite mistaken ideas. Obvious examples of a wide class are provided by advertisements of patent medicines and of goods which will improve the appearance or charm of the purchaser. Not quite so wasteful, but still comparable to the window-breaking glazier, are advertisements which 'create' transitory demands, unless it can be maintained that we are pleased by a succession of novelties of which we shall soon grow weary.

Criticism of a similar kind may be directed against the devices of intensive salesmanship, by which a salesman induces a purchaser to buy something more expensive than he intended, or conceals from him the fact that cheaper articles are available than those actually shown. Here what is bought is worth in the market the price charged, but, so far as pressure has been brought on the customer it is not worth the price to him; hence the transaction is not as useful an exchange as it might have been. The sellers as a class are in the same position as before, since only the same total amount is available to spend; but some of their efforts have been misdirected, since the customer has less for his money than he might have had.

In the relations between employer and employee further examples can be found. As we have seen, the presumption of competition is that the employer should give as little, and the employee obtain as much, as can be paid; for it is only as the result of such a bargaining process that there can be the most economic distribution of labour among employments. But after the contract of service has been made the case is changed, for both sides have agreed, the one to give and the other to receive a certain amount of work; and methods which depend on the ignorance of either party in order to give or to get other amounts than this are of the nature of deceptions. From the employee's side, this may take the form of doing or omitting to do things which will 'not be noticed', and in general doing less than the best work possible. This is particularly dangerous for those in positions of responsibility, who have to set their own standards to a large extent; and for the servants of large businesses and of Government departments who are tempted to be unduly lavish with the resources which they control, while sparing of their own efforts. For the employee, the criterion of fairness is not what he can extort from his employer, but what he agreed to do when he was engaged.

The practice of 'ca' canny' or 'going slow' demands special consideration, since it is often adopted from a sense of loyalty to fellow workers, either through a desire not to set them too high a standard, or because it is thought that the work available will be spread out if it is done slowly, and the demand for labour thus improved. Where a particular class of labour has a monopoly this end may actually be secured, but the same objection applies to this as to all other monopolistic practices, to which we shall refer in a moment. In general, however, the effect is to reduce the output of the worker and to make the position of the employer more difficult: his capacity to demand labour and to pay wages depends on his success as a producer, and the economic interest of the whole community is served by efficient production. There can be no doubt that if every one worked less there would be less produced and therefore less to consume. It is the same with the objection to the introduction of machinery. We feel ourselves bound to sympathize with men who are thrown out of work for this reason, and who can hardly be expected to consider the interests of the community while their own families are in danger of privation. Yet we cannot doubt that the advances made in the technique of machine

production in the last century have caused a large increase in the standard of living in industrial countries,
and lightened the tasks and shortened the hours of
all workers. To set our faces against the development
of machines is to turn against a movement which
affords the best hope of a solution of the whole economic problem.

On the employer's side, the chief danger of course
is that he will exploit the weakness rather than the
ignorance of his workers. Nevertheless, and speaking generally, an employer is acting in the common
interest when he pays no more for a piece of work
than he need; for while there is competition the ultimate effects of his profits will be to lower the price of
his product to the public, or to increase the wages
he must pay if he is to keep his men. When there
is unemployment, it is particularly the case that
he does better to take on extra hands than to raise
the wages of his men if he is being successful. It
hardly needs to be said that it is advantageous to
every one to treat employees as well as is compatible
with efficiency, and to pay them what is necessary to
keep them in the same employment: there is an increasing recognition everywhere that this is a matter
of sound business policy as well as of humanity.

But where the worker can be exploited through
his ignorance the same principles will apply. It is, of
course, directly dishonest to manipulate piece-work
scales or rates of measurement; but to conceal from
a worker that his services are satisfactory or valuable,

to lay burdens on him because he will not refuse them, or to pay him less than his cost of replacement because he is not aware of this : all these are not in the spirit of fair exchanges.

The exercise of monopolistic power, which occurs when a group or an individual controls all the buying or selling of a particular commodity, is also against the general interest. In a seller's monopoly supply is restricted, and the public have to pay more than would otherwise be necessary; while in a buyer's monopoly an exchange which is unfair to the weaker party can be dictated. A state has no business to charge monopoly prices unless they are intended as a convenient form of taxation. For although, in the case of monopolies established or supported by the state, there is usually some regard for the public welfare, a scheme of restriction not meant to assist the revenue is usually no more than an awkward or indolent device to ease or to avoid adjustments which free competition would bring about too drastically. When some part of an existing output has to be destroyed, as has been done for example with Brazilian coffee, or when plant is kept idle or output limited, as in the case of the British coal scheme, we have something very like a confession of failure. Though dislocation is in itself likely to cause hardship, an attempt should be made as soon as possible to use the surplus capacity for some other form of production. Any continuing necessity of destroying what has been produced is offensively wasteful when there

is still so much poverty, and to keep resources idle
is little better.

Apart from state action, individuals are often in a
position in which they can exert some monopoly
power. It is indeed unusual to find individual workers
who can improve their income by deliberately re-
stricting the amount they do; professional men with
special abilities are more often overworked because
of their public activities—for example, great doctors
who spend part of their time in public hospitals.
Where they do less than is within their power, they
are withholding something of special value; it is a
public virtue for them to work too hard, and a public
disservice to do too little. But in any case, as it is
difficult to be conspicuously successful without overwork, there is not much danger that any professional
man will be able to establish such a monopoly of his
services as to exploit the public.

The case is different, however, when there are
groups of sellers who restrict their production. Although there is often legislation against the activities
of such groups, they are hard to define and harder to
control. But though we cannot give an exact defini-
tion of fair profits, there are many occasions on which
we can with confidence say that they are too high.
Perhaps a test can be found by a consideration of the
circumstances which prevent competition from acting in any particular case. If there is an actual scarcity
so that everything which can be produced is on the
market, there is no monopoly. And when, as is often

the case with middlemen who seem to be making
high charges for what they do, other people could
enter the business and do not do so, the charges cannot be more than enough to make it worth while
giving the services. But where a monopoly is maintained by the strength of the firm which has secured
it, so that it adopts special tactics against would-be
rivals, there is a clear divergence between private and
public welfare.

Labour organizations, especially those formed
among professional and skilled workers, may also
act as monopolists. This may be done by restrict-
ing entry into the occupation by high entrance fees,
or by apprenticeship regulations or examinations
more severe than are required to keep up the necessary standard of skill. There is a sense no doubt in
which we can say that all wages ought to be equal;
but we ought to add that in computing their equality
allowance must be made for differences in skill, cost
of training, and intrinsic attractiveness. These differences can be measured with some precision, and if
(after they have been reckoned with) particular kinds
of labour obtain higher rates than would be required
to obtain a supply of suitable labour if there were no
organization, there is a monopolistic element which
operates unfavourably against other workers and the
public. Where all workers together insist on rates so
high that they cannot all be employed except at a loss,
then those who remain at work are acting as monopolists against the community in general—their own

gain as members of the community is less than the others' losses, and the action is anti-social.

The objection to a buyer's monopoly is that the weaker party to the transaction loses more than is gained by the stronger. Competition, if it were perfect, would operate to end arrangements like this, but its working is often inadequate. Common examples of the buyer's monopoly are the agreements among dealers attending sales, which certainly exist despite legal prohibition. But in almost all transactions, those who possess knowledge and money are likely to be able to drive hard bargains because of the ignorance and the necessity of the weak and the poor. We have already considered the case of bargains carried out when one of the bargainers is ignorant. Employers in general have a sort of buyer's monopoly, because of the difficulty which their employees find in obtaining a new position. This is particularly the case with married and elderly employees, who can be forced to endure conditions and treatment which they need not have accepted if they had been in a position to wait. The infliction of uncertainty is an exercise of monopoly which is cruel though sometimes unconscious. No one who has ever experienced uncertainty about anything of real importance will deny that it is an evil; and among the poorer sections of the community it reaches an intensity almost unknown to those who have never been uncertain about the next meal of their dependants. All this calls our attention again to the peculiar responsibility which rests on the owners of property. They compete, it is true, with one another: but not with sufficient severity to prevent them all together enjoying a privileged situation at the expense of those who have none.

It must not be supposed that all dealers should pay for what they buy at exactly the rates at which they will sell again; or that workers should be paid exactly the amounts at which their products will sell. For if this were so it would not be worth while to be a dealer or employer. But the purpose of exchanges is that both sides should gain from them, and the best exchange is that which benefits both sides equally. Though it is hard to be precise about the conception of fairness, it remains true that the tests of it are concerned with equality of knowledge and bargaining power.

Our original proposition, that we are satisfying the most intense needs we are able to, when we do what brings us in the highest return available, has now been qualified by the stipulation that the transactions should have the elusive but real quality of fairness. We must now consider the proposition still further, and to do this we must try to find out what money really measures. Though it is certainly not happiness, money gives command of commodities with which our material needs may be satisfied, and it follows that with a larger amount of it more of these will be satisfied. To live at all we must have some income, and to have even the possibility of happiness, self-development, or whatever is our aim in life, most of us need a larger income than would suffice for bare necessities. It is this which leads almost every one to choose from among otherwise similar courses the one which brings in the greater monetary return. No one will maintain that to be twice as rich as before is to be twice as happy. But the richer man has more possibilities than the poorer, and the lower the scales of income with which we are dealing, the more likely is it that this will be true. And since the majority of men have small incomes there is a strong presumption that the individual who produces most wealth, by adding most to the common stock, is helping most to make his goods cheap for every one: while (if we do not consider at this point how the incomes are distributed) the largest contribution means the greatest possibility from the wealth thus produced.

We must now ask whether all kinds of valuable goods are conducive to human welfare to an extent proportionate to their price. In one sense, it is clear that they are not. We should suffer more from the loss of *all* our food than from the loss of anything else which cost the same amount. But when we consider the last amount, say the last shilling, spent on each kind of purchase, we seem to be attempting to get the same satisfaction from each different use. If I got more satisfaction from a shilling spent on beer than from one spent on cider, I could improve my position by diverting some of my expenditure on the latter to the former. We do this very badly for ourselves, but the fact that we so often realize that we could have laid

out our income in a better way shows that we are trying to make the most of it, and this is secured when
each of our final shillings on different things gives
equal satisfaction.

Thus it is argued that all wants leading to similar
monetary demands are as good as one another so far
as happiness is concerned: the fact that some one is
willing to buy a thing shows that he wants it at least
as much as anything else he could have got for the
money. This may be a circular argument ethically,
but we should be cautious about attacking it as a practical test of wants, which are very individual in their
character. Toleration is essential for progress, and
though we may be ready to tell others what they ought
to desire, we do not like them to treat us in this way.
Yet when our desires or actions interfere with the
liberties of others a distinction can and must be made:
both law and morality try to prevent the individual
pursuing his own ends at the expense of his fellows.
For various reasons the law is imperfect, and it then
becomes necessary ourselves to consider our actions
from this point of view. If they are indifferent, then
the most profitable course is best. If they are beneficial to others, there is an added reason for doing
them. But if they are harmful, the damage to others
should be counted as against the gain to ourselves.

Thus all actions which are both legal and profitable,
but which have incidental effects which do not show
themselves in the form of monetary gains or losses
to the parties to the transactions, may be weighed

with these considerations in mind. It is difficult to make an exact classification, and we should be cautious in criticizing the behaviour of others, but if we are convinced that their actions are injurious we must not take refuge in 'minding our own business'. Smoky chimneys, garden walls which obscure the view, unnecessary noise are all convenient examples of actions which damage, disturb, or annoy others and thus take something from them. On the other side we may find actions, such as opening a private park to the public, in which the community benefits at little expense to the person concerned. In our private affairs we try to take account of incidental effects of this kind, and we should do the same in our business transactions.

The utmost caution is needed either in conducting or in criticizing businesses which please some people and irritate others. It is common experience that some forms of satisfaction are more enduring than others and that some are marred by subsequent regrets. When we act with sufficient deliberation we take these factors into account, but we do not always do so. Hence the state can and does compel children and adults to do things which they do not want to do, and prevents them from doing things which they would do, at least as much in their own interests as in those of the public generally. But in the last resort every one who is neither inexperienced nor feeble-minded must be the judge of his own good; and it can be argued that the state should not prohibit or compel any activity affecting the individual alone if he is of an age or capacity to form considered opinions.

Yet in choosing our occupations there is surely some duty upon us, not to put ourselves in the position of suppliers of commodities which experience shows that the purchasers are likely to regret, however willing they may be to pay profitable prices. For neither the state nor the seller finds it possible to distinguish the experienced from the callow, the strong-minded from the weak. I do not say that we should condemn all activities which are open to abuse, for we are all prone to think that what we do not like is at best useless, and that what we do like is really best for others if they could be brought to see the light. But the supply of facilities of certain kinds, of which drinking and gambling are the commonest examples, may very well assist others to make themselves objectionable, and offer a particular temptation to the inexperienced; hence a special responsibility rests upon those who choose to provide these facilities. The worst harm that can come from ordinary forms of production is that they may make something too plentiful and something else too scarce—if an occupation can easily entail doing greater harm than this we should be reluctant to enter it.

The opposite course would be to enter an occupation of less than average profitability because it is unusually advantageous to the community. If we do this because we like it, the gain to ourselves is a sort of direct production of satisfaction which from our

point of view offsets the monetary loss. But the case
of men who enter unpaid or badly paid occupations
from a sense of duty is important. It is clear that no
rules can be laid down for the performance of such
voluntary work, no calculus made by which we may
even guess about it. We cannot say how much self-
sacrifice by a doctor, for example, in a leper colony,
is equivalent to so much welfare received by the inhabitants, for we are dealing with considerations to
which no measure is applicable. But an enormous
addition is made to the welfare of the community
every year by the voluntary work of those who feel
it to be their duty to their neighbours. Examples can
be found everywhere—the work done by hospitals,
by educational associations, by societies for providing cultural facilities and for maintaining open spaces,
and a great variety of work which seeks to improve
standards of living. Those who have an adequate income from property have special opportunities in
this way.

Such voluntary workers are sustained by the conviction that they are right, and do not need any
theories to support or to criticize them. Yet we cannot doubt that much effort is wasted or misdirected
because of the unquestioning acceptance of certain
ends as universally beneficial. Every one who wishes
to do what he can in this way should consider two
things. First, whether a proposed change can be
brought about without causing unwanted incidental
changes—thus the systems of many native races have

been upset in ways which have destroyed their lives altogether, by those who wished to confer some particular benefit upon them. And second, when the proposed change is not wanted by those to whom it is proposed, there is a heavy responsibility on those who attempt to bring it about—they must justify themselves by results, since failure is not only a waste of their own efforts but a negative contribution because of the interference with others.

In any case, we are now moving far from the field in which economic reasoning can be applied. Such reasoning is only valid where welfare of an economic kind is under consideration; where, that is, an improvement in the situation of some section of people is sought, of a kind which is obtainable by the expenditure of money. Thus the provision of drainage or electricity, though the recipients at present prefer to spend their money on other things, may well be justified if they realize later that the new forms of expenditure are worth while. And the same may be said of attempts to improve the health, the marketing, or the cooking of the public, to take examples at random. Anything which economizes effort or material, or which satisfies existing wants more simply or effectively, is *prima facie* desirable from an economic point of view, whether it appears to be wanted or not. For we must assume that reasonable men would choose in accordance with these criteria were the full facts before them. But much voluntary effort is directed towards effecting alterations in the aesthetic, the cultural, and the spiritual satisfactions of the community, and in these values, the exchange value is only an incidental constituent, for each must stand or fall primarily in its own right. A man who chooses to devote his life to the development of the musical appreciation of his fellows does not help his case very much if he shows that music, when understood, is an inexpensive recreation, nor is he harmed irretrievably in it, if it is shown that the time given to music causes a material loss.

Having now considered some of the possible effects on others of the way we earn our incomes, we must consider what happens when we spend it. By spending money on anything we encourage its production, and thus we should be careful whenever we feel inclined to buy something which may be harmless to us, but the production or use of which may damage some one else. There are cases in which it is very difficult to decide : it may only worsen the position of workers in an underpaid trade if we refuse to buy its products. Where this aspect is not present, then we must remember what has been called 'the controlling power of demand'. To buy goods which we suspect to have been smuggled or stolen, or even to buy anything in hours when its sale is prohibited, is to encourage others in law-breaking, even though we ourselves keep on the right side of the law. In the same way it may be argued that if we object to performing animals, or to hazardous employments, it is irrational to attend circuses or to buy the products of such employ-

ments. Again, there are occupations which offer
temptations to the weak or inexperienced; and if I
patronize them, I am making it easier for these others
to succumb to temptation, even though I myself am
proof against it. No clear lines can be drawn: we cannot say how much weight we should attach to the advantages of allowing free choice to all; and how much
to the disadvantages of allowing it to those not yet
mature. But we ought at least to know what we are
doing when we spend our incomes.

Personal expenditure may also have effects on the
feelings of others. This is largely a question of good
manners. We can all do a great deal by 'doing as we
would be done by', rather than insisting on our rights
to do as we choose. Conspicuous expenditure, meant
to show in public the superior wealth of the spender,
is one of the reasons for objecting to inequalities of
income. Thoughtless spending by the rich cannot be
desirable in the presence of poverty; and extrava-
gance among people of the same social class but with
different incomes sets standards which are maintained
with great difficulty. The remedy ought to be the
choice of a more suitable set of conventions, but until this counsel of perfection has been taken the richer
can help their neighbours at small inconvenience to
themselves.

Finally we come to the most difficult and unsatisfactory part of our subject, the sharing of income
with others by the individual to whom it belongs.
If we all received amounts proportionate to our

needs there would be some grounds for saying that this was the best distribution, but it is clearly impossible to agree on a standard of needs. It cannot be proved, indeed, that any particular distribution is better than any other; few, however, will deny that the rich would suffer less from the loss of their superfluities, as soon as they became accustomed to their deprivation, than the poor would gain from an increase in what Ricardo called their 'moderate comforts'.

For a number of reasons, of which this is one, those who are Socialists work for a society in which there shall be much more equality. They hope that motives of a social character will eventually displace to a large extent the present inducements to work, which are mostly monetary. At present it is comparatively rare to find men who work their utmost entirely for social reasons; and if every one were to be given the same income irrespective of the quantity or quality of his output, it is likely that there would be a general loss of efficiency, so that the position of the average man would be worse than it now is. Indeed, it is not easy to show that if we all received the same incomes the efficient would nevertheless be under an obligation to produce more than the inefficient. So that even if we think that equal incomes would be best, we ought not to want others to have them until we have persuaded a majority to do their best irrespective of the return they get.

Yet there is still a presumption in favour of the

view that more use can be made of a small income
than of the same amount added to a large one : every
contribution from the large for the relief of the small
will have at least the potentiality of bringing more
satisfaction than it takes away. All the great moral
teachers of the world have laid stress on the duty of
those with large possessions, and a decision on this
point is the hardest of those we are commonly called
upon to make. Unless we can bring ourselves to
believe that inequality of incomes is a sort of physical
necessity, an inescapable condition of human existence, we must face the problem of how much we
should give away.

Having decided how much to give, we must decide
also how to give. Here I think that it is clear that the
most useful assistance is that which supplements
efforts already being made by the person helped, and
in particular those which with assistance will be successful. For there can be no duty on us to reduce our
own standards in order to allay a want which the person who feels it makes no effort to satisfy. If it is
doubtful (as some people say) whether we ought to
keep alive those who will never be able to help themselves, it is quite certain that the vicious and the depraved should at least supply themselves with the
means for their excesses.

This concludes our hurried survey of the ways in
which our activities in getting and spending our incomes affect the situation of others. There is no need
for us to 'lay waste our powers', as Wordsworth

feared. Many of us will never find ourselves in situations where we shall do much active harm. But if we try, as we should in all questions of personal ethics, to consider the feelings and interests of all those who may be affected by our activities, it is easy to make a positive contribution to the well-being of society.

VI. GAMBLING

By R. C. MORTIMER

ON the question of gambling opinion is divided. Some class it among the vices, others among the amusements. For some it is a thing which conscience can never sanction; for others, it is like oysters or seed-cake—legitimate enough if you happen to like that kind of thing. But the question is one of some importance in these days, because the practice of gambling has become so widespread. It is as though many persons were making oysters or seed-cake their sole and staple diet. On any such scale, gambling is agreed by all to be an evil, and the existence of this admittedly 'evil' gambling has raised the question whether the practice in itself is inherently and necessarily 'evil', or whether the 'evil' we deplore is simply a regrettable abuse of an otherwise harmless amusement.

It is certain that the legitimacy of gambling would never have been called in question if it were not for the frequency with which it leads to moral or financial ruin. And the discussion of the question has been largely confused by a tendency to equate gambling as such, with that form of gambling which produces those consequences, and to use the term 'gambling' in the sense of disastrous or ruinous gambling.[1] Once pointed out, this is immediately seen to be a begging

[1] See my *Gambling*, pp. 26 ff.

of the question, which leaves entirely unsettled the problem of whether gambling which has not led to these consequences is immoral.

There are two main grounds on which it is held that any gamble must be immoral. First, that it is immoral to make the ownership of property dependent on chance; and second, that it is immoral to get something for which one gives nothing in return.

The first of these arguments has considerable strength. Chance is of the essence of any gamble; this is true no matter to what extent the element of skill may enter in as well. For the moment that skill so predominates in the matter as to make it certain that skill ultimately decides the issue to the exclusion of chance, then by common consent the matter ceases to be a gamble. The playing of bridge for money is regarded as a gamble only so long as the skill of the two sides is so evenly balanced that the ultimate decision rests with the luck of the cards. If it is not so, then the more skilful pair regard the matter not as a gamble, but as a lucrative employment, and their victims regard it at best as an expensive lesson.

But it will probably not be disputed that by a gamble is meant a transaction in which the ownership of some piece of property is made wholly or partially dependent on chance. The opponents of gambling maintain that such a procedure is a dishonour to reason and treachery to civilization. One of the chief functions (they point out) of the practical reason is to foresee and to forestall the future: the chief success of civilization has been to protect men from the catastrophes of sudden chance events. Civilization, the possibility of an ordered settled life, rests on a feeling of security. And this feeling of security is acquired and maintained by reason, which, working with the instrument of cause and effect, minimizes so far as possible the uncertain and the unknown.

The evidences of this effort and achievement are to be seen on all sides, in man's control—or partial control—of his environment. The advances of medical science have been inspired by the wish to prevent premature death, to ward off plagues and epidemics, and, in general, by the removal in the sphere of health of the uncertain and the unpredictable, to give to every individual a reasonable expectation of a normal span of life. The elaborate system of insurance has had a similar aim in the sphere of property. The whole material prosperity of the individual is no longer subject to destruction by a single chance event. Where, in the old days, a trader stood to lose everything in a shipwreck, now by an even distribution of risks over a wide area the loss is shared, and so prevented from involving him in ruin. The efforts of Trade Unions are directed towards securing permanence of employment, independent of the chance whim of an employer or the transitory conditions of the markets. It is the aim of the Socialist party on the one hand, and of the Socialist element in the Fascist and Nazi doctrines on the other, to ensure that the possession of wealth or opportunity shall not depend on the chance accident

of birth, but that all men being given an equal opportunity, or all being pressed into the service of the
commonwealth, the rewards shall be apportioned according to merit. Since then it is the whole work and
business of civilization to eliminate as far as possible
the operations of mere chance, to make men independent of the unknown and the unpredictable, how can
it be right arbitrarily and unnecessarily to reintroduce
that element?

I say unnecessarily, because not only cannot chance
be completely eliminated, but on certain occasions it is
necessary to appeal to it, and to invoke risk. Certain
branches of trade, for instance, could not be carried
on without speculations about future prices; and
those speculations necessarily involve a large element of uncertainty. Moreover every great advance
in human progress has been preceded by the taking
of risks on the part of the pioneers. The opening up
of remoter parts of the globe, and the exploitation of
mineral wealth are obvious instances; and it would
not be difficult to think of a great many others. In
general a risk is judged to be necessary or justifiable,
(1) when every effort has been made by the reason to
minimize the extent of the unknown, (2) when the
advantage hoped for is commensurate with the loss
risked (i.e. it would be unjustifiable to risk one's life
to save a sparrow, but justifiable to risk it to save a
child), and (3) when the probability of a favourable
outcome is greater than the probability of an unfavourable one. If this last condition is not fulfilled,

we are apt to call it not a risk but a danger or at any rate a grave risk. A grave risk is never justifiable except where the second condition is amply fulfilled, i.e. where what we stand to gain is of pressing and supreme importance.

It is then only to introduce the element of chance *unnecessarily* which we regard as wrong; and this is what gambling always does. To introduce it in such a way as unnecessarily to endanger our *whole* livelihood on the preceding argument must be wrong. For to do so is a deliberate attempt to destroy what reason and civilization are trying to build up—security of life. But is it equally wrong to endanger even *part* of our livelihood in this way?

That is not so clear. In a world from which chance has been completely eliminated, in a world from which it has been eliminated even to the extent to which it has to-day, there is a very real danger of monotony. Not the monotony which results from the continued performance of the same activities—that we can always in some measure avoid. But the monotony which comes from the absence of any element of surprise, the monotony which obtains where nothing can ever happen but what we ourselves cause to happen, where we are never exposed to events and experiences which are beyond our own control—from this monotony gambling affords a refuge. And it is in part as a refuge of this kind that gambling is so largely practised at the present time.

As an antidote to monotony of this kind gambling

has a justification. But only as an antidote, a stimulant, a recreation, an amusement. It should not be made the main business of life. For that would indeed be a dishonour to reason, a treachery to civilization. But as a means of reintroducing, to a limited extent—limited by reason—that element of chance which has been banished from the main interests of life, it is justified. For risk in moderation acts as a mental stimulant, and much of the fun of life comes from the presence of the unexpected. What most men, I imagine, would really like, is a complete certainty about the security and stability of the things that matter, together with uncertainty about the comparatively unimportant. The game of cricket would be futile if no one obeyed the rules, but on the other hand that which makes it, we are told, the greatest of games and raises it so incomparably far above all others is its 'glorious uncertainty'.

Within a limited sphere, where it can do no harm to the serious business of life, it is no more wrong to play with chance, than, within the limited sphere of team games, it is wrong to play with the war spirit. Team games are miniature imitations of war. They are an expression of group loyalty. Within strictly enforced limits they allow an outlet for those instincts and emotions which on the grand scale of real life produce class and national wars. As providing such harmless outlets they are of incalculable value. Gambling, if reason strictly enforces its proper limits, provides a similar outlet for the desire of excitement which, deprived of the outlet afforded by that complete rule of chance which obtained more or less in primitive times, might now find some other more disastrous one. It was, I think, Alexander the Great who said that so long as his soldiers were gamblers he felt secure against mutiny. If then a man likes to find his amusement in gambling, he is as much entitled to spend his money on it as he is on cinemas or football matches. The fact that he may spend too much money is no more a condemnation of the one than it is of the other.

But gambling is condemned on another ground, besides that of the appeal to chance. It is argued that the gambler gets something for nothing, and that that must be wrong. Without going into the question of whether the principle here is right—and if it is right it would seem at first sight to throw doubt on the legitimacy of receiving a gift[1]—it is enough to say that in fact the gambler does *not* get something for nothing. In the gambling contract certain rights are mutually conferred. In the event of one set of circumstances A gives B the right to claim from him a sum of money: in the event of certain other circumstances B gives A a similar right. It cannot be maintained that this conferring of a right is nothing; it is a definite contribution, in virtue of which the gambler earns—becomes entitled to—his winnings. On the other hand it is maintained by the opponents of gambling that, since by the terms of the contract both claims

[1] See *Gambling*, p. 68.

cannot be substantiated, the contribution of the winner in fact amounts to nothing—that compared with
the material gain of the winner this temporary and
unsubstantiated claim of the loser may properly be
regarded as nothing.

But even if this be granted, yet the immorality of
the contract has still not been proved. The insurance
contract is of precisely the same nature. If I insure the
contents of my house against burglary, the insurance
company makes a bet with me. If in the course of the
year I am burgled, the company will make good my
losses; if I have no burglary I shall have paid them a
premium and got nothing in return. That is, there is
a contract by the terms of which, in certain circumstances they confer a right on me, in certain other
circumstances I confer a right on them and it is
impossible for both of us to substantiate our claims.
Where is the difference between that and the gambling
contract?

The difference, it is said, lies here. (1) The insurance companies render a useful service to the community. They distribute the risks. (2) They afford
a sense of security; the premium which the individual
pays each year is a just price for that peace of mind
which this security gives him. But this is to introduce
a quite different consideration. We are no longer
comparing the material gain of the winner with the
material loss of the loser, but we are setting against
a material gain a mental or spiritual asset. But the
gambler can claim to do that equally well. If the

person who takes out an insurance policy buys therewith peace of mind, the gambler who purchases a
sweepstake ticket buys therewith a pleasurable mental
excitement. If the one is justified, why not the other?
And as regards the first point, if the insurance company is justified because it serves the community
by distributing risks, may not the 'bookie' and the
sweepstake promoter equally claim that they serve
the community by distributing pleasure? They take
rank with the proprietors of cinema halls as caterers
for the public amusement.

This argument, therefore, cannot be used to condemn gambling as a whole. It is reduced to the claim
that the gambler gets a disproportionate return for
his money. But it is obviously a matter of difficult
individual assessment to say how much material loss
is a fair return for the excitement provided, and it may
often happen that the winner gets no more than the
loser is prepared to pay. In any case it is no argument,
as it stands, against gambling as a whole, but only
against gambling with too high stakes.

To be effective as an argument against gambling as
a whole it would have to rest either on the principle
that to do the opposite of an insurance—i.e. unnecessarily to incur a risk—is wrong, or on the principle
that the kind of pleasure which a gamble provides
is itself immoral. The first principle we have already
dealt with. It is not necessarily immoral arbitrarily
to incur a risk. The second remains. And it is
probably this which lies at the bottom of that

hatred which many serious-minded persons feel for all forms of gambling.

'The sort of pleasure which the gambling thrill gives is wrong.' It is not the taking of risks. That may often be necessary and beneficial. It is not the mere excitement of it—that is no worse than many other external stimuli, from a glass of wine to the reading of a detective novel, but it is the close connexion which exists between this particular thrill and the desire for gain. There lies its danger—there its wrongness.

It is idle to deny that the anticipation of gain is an indispensable element in the pleasure of gambling. Those who say that they gamble purely for the fun of it, and do not care whether they win or lose, talk nonsense. They may not care much, but they do care. For the particular nature of the thrill of gambling consists in the suspense and uncertainty as to whether we shall lose or win *something*. And it is a fact that where winnings are prohibited—if, e.g., they are confiscated for charity—gambling dwindles or dies. Nor is that surprising. You might as well expect people to continue going to the cinema when they are presented only with educational films, as that a man should go on gambling without standing to win anything. For as the object of the one is the excitement to be found in watching a story—an excitement of a particular kind—so the object of the other is the excitement to be found in winning a prize.

It is this close connexion with the desire for money

which makes gambling so odious to many people. It is regarded by them as a form of avarice, and an incitement to selfishness. And such, no doubt, it very often is. Where the desire for gain so predominates in the whole business as completely to destroy the element of relaxation and amusement, gambling is wrong, because it is then regarded solely as a means of making money, and from that point of view it is both foolish and unreasonable. Steady employment is at once a more probable and a more beneficial way of acquiring one's living, than is the backing of problematic winners. And even if one is successful and does back the winners, still that is no proper substitute for work. Where, however, the desire for gain does not predominate, but is only allied with a desire for amusement and relaxation, its immorality is not so clear. For there is nothing wrong in the desire for gain in itself. Everybody desires a return for his work and his money, and everybody desires to receive a present. We only condemn people for having these desires, when they have them to the exclusion of everything else, when they are 'obsessed' by them.

So that, if a gamble be indulged in solely for the sake of the possible winnings, it might be condemned, on the ground that it is then regarded as a substitute for work, but if it be indulged in primarily for fun, only part of which fun lies in the lively expectation of gain, it would appear to be legitimate. And, except in the case of professional punters, most gambling is probably of this nature. That is, it has as its aims the provision of the twofold pleasure of a gratifying surprise. While we are young, surprises of one kind or another are not infrequent. For an adult they are rare: people do not often give him unexpected presents. But the desire for them persists. By indulging in a gamble he places himself in the position of being a possible recipient of one. The desire for it, the desire of gain, is undoubtedly present in his mind, and yet it is the fun of it, the excitement of being in that position, quite as much as the desire of the gain itself, which prompts the entry into the gambling contract. From that fun or excitement he derives a mental stimulus which gives to the gamble a value of its own, quite apart from the winning of any material gain. The desire for gain, in itself not immoral, does not necessarily in every gamble become so excessive as to make the gamble vicious.

That this is so is shown by the fact that the disappointed gambler does not as a rule grudge the winner his gains. With the exception of those who are gambling to excess, the gambler, though disappointed, does not regret having made the gamble. He bought a chance knowing it was only a chance, and the result was what he always knew it might be. Discontent, unrest, and envy do not necessarily result at all. If they do, they are signs that the gambler entered into a gamble in the wrong spirit, and beyond his means; and such gambling no doubt is wrong. But there is a great deal of gambling in which these factors do not result at all. All that happens is that an innocent desire to receive a present and an innocent desire for a little excitement are allowed expression.

I am convinced, therefore, that within limits indulgence in gambling is legitimate. Where it does not endanger those essentials of livelihood—food, clothes, house, maintenance, and education of children, higher amusements and recreations—which it is the business of reason to safeguard against chance, and where it does not become an obsession, occupying a disproportionate amount of one's time and attention, it fills legitimately enough a humble position in the economy of our lives, side by side with the watching of football matches and the attendance at picture houses.

But there is one other aspect of the matter which deserves attention. If all things are lawful, it may be that not all things are expedient. Just at present gambling is perhaps the most popular national amusement. While the mere statement of the quite enormous sum of money which annually changes hands as the result of gambling is no proof that the gambling is excessive (for it may be, as some people contend, that very few persons actually spend on it more than they can afford), yet the opinion of those who are best able to judge is unanimous that much harm is being done. 'We have been impressed by the spread of organized facilities for betting and gambling and of the habit of betting and gambling. The weight of the evidence shows that serious social consequences are ensuing.'[1]

[1] *Interim Report of the Royal Commission on Lotteries and Betting*, Dec. 1932.

Against the united testimony of social workers of
every kind, clergy, nurses, government departments,
police, it is idle to argue that no problem exists, or that
the gambling which goes on in the country represents
only a legitimate expenditure of pocket-money. If
anything is certain, it is that a great deal of excessive
gambling is going on. I only stress this really very
obvious fact, because one meets so many people who
protest that there is nothing to worry about. The
situation is indeed a serious one. And it owes its
existence to the vast amount of organized gambling
facilities afforded to the public.

Legislation is needed and, no doubt, will shortly
be put in hand, not indeed to take away the Englishman's right to gamble if he wants to, but to limit his
opportunities of gambling to excess. In a strong community such legislation would no doubt be both unnecessary and insulting, but where a malady is proved
a remedy must be provided. Gambling is always a
dangerous amusement lending itself very readily to
excess. And if a great number have fallen victims to
that excess they must be rescued, and others must be
prevented from going the same way, if necessary
against their wills. Restrictions on their liberty are a
sacrifice which the strong must make in the interests
of the weak. It is a principle which we admit and obey
in the case of the sale of alcohol. It must also be applied to the provision of facilities for gambling. Some
limitation of the number of horse and greyhound racecourses, and of the number of racing days on each,

must be laid down. The dissemination of betting news through the public press, and the creation, through the medium of clubs and public houses, of more or less public centres of betting must be controlled. Such legislation is inspired not by Puritanism but by the principle of good government. In the interests both of the commonwealth and of the individual such measures as are possible must be taken to prevent and discourage the individual from falling into excess. Strict legislation for a generation would probably succeed in canalizing the gambling instinct into proper and legitimate outlets. Mere repression would be useless, and if attempted would prove disastrous. Prohibition in America is an example of the wrong method. Limitation and guidance are required.

In this connexion the question of sweepstakes is often raised. Would it not be in the public interest for the state to run periodic lotteries, and, whilst providing this outlet, to prohibit or drastically reduce most other forms of organized gambling? Whether under those conditions laws forbidding or limiting public betting on racecourses, and the publication of betting news in the press, would have a chance of being enforced is a practical question which it might be of some interest to debate. At first sight it seems unlikely. Men might still prefer to bet on horse-races and football matches rather than in a lottery; and if so why should they not? And how could you effectively prevent them? In that case, the only result of state lotteries would be to add one more to the existing facilities for gambling. On the other hand, it might be argued that men only want to gamble, and do not much mind what they gamble about, so that either by penalizing other forms, or making state lotteries especially attractive, you could easily wean them from the one form to the other. And then you would have this advantage, that by limiting the number of lotteries and the size of the prizes and the price of the tickets, the state would be in a position to exercise effective control.

But whatever the merits of these two arguments, the question, in fact, is hardly ever debated along these lines. It generally turns on the question whether sweepstakes and lotteries are moral or not, and whether the state ought to encourage them and derive revenue from them. As far as the first is concerned, perhaps enough has been said already. One might perhaps add that as a way of raising money for charity they are wasteful and pernicious. Wasteful, because of the high cost of organization, pernicious because of the unholy alliance between altruism and self-seeking. For this attempt to bribe people to subscribe to charities by an appeal to their self-interest, there is nothing to be said. It is an insult to charity, and a source of offence because it tends to blunt men's consciences. It obscures for them the realization that it is their plain duty to give alms in any case, wholly and completely without consideration of any hopes they may entertain of doing good to themselves thereby. To wheedle men into subscribing by offering them brilliant hopes is to lower our moral standard; to flatter them with the pretence that they are being charitable, when in fact they are amusing themselves, is hypocrisy.

But considered as an amusement pure and simple lotteries are justifiable. And perhaps of all forms of gambling they are the most innocuous, since their number can be limited, and the stake is fixed. The serious objection to state lotteries as they are run in other countries, and to the Irish sweepstakes, lies in the size of the prizes awarded. To win as much as £30,000 by a single chance removes the whole affair out of the category of amusements. It affects the whole structure of a man's life. It is a surrender to the sole arbitration of chance of the condition which determines one's whole life. And as such it is as much open to objection as to risk the *loss* of one's livelihood in gambling is. As far as the appeal to chance goes, it is the same thing. It is also against the public interest; for wealth so easily and suddenly acquired brings with it little sense of responsibility. And it is in flagrant contradiction both to the Socialist principle that wealth should be proportionate to merit, and to the Conservative principle that wealth should be entailed in those families who have become trained and accustomed to use it as trustees of the public interest. But if lottery prizes were so limited as to bear some proportion to the price of the ticket and so to resemble more the receipt of a present than the inheritance of a fortune, little moral objection, I think, could be found to them. And this further advantage would be added that, with the same funds to be disposed of, a greater number of people would secure prizes and the consequent happiness would be more widely distributed.

But though state lotteries with small prizes might be the most satisfactory form of public gambling in certain circumstances, the present moment, with our existing laws and the national temper what it is, is not the one for introducing them. What we need is not more facilities but fewer. Nothing must be done which would appear to give public encouragement to gambling, but rather the reverse. The swollen extent of the present facilities is no doubt chiefly due to the public demand, and they can never satisfactorily be reduced by law alone. The demand must first be lessened. There is room here for a self-denying ordinance on the part of all conscientious persons who feel seriously in the matter. Before patronizing any public form of gambling, whether by sweepstake or 'bookies', they ought to ask and answer in all earnestness the question 'Does not even one single contribution help to swell the demand, and keep alive a public evil?' It seems to me that, if they feel the present facilities for gambling to be excessive, they cannot in conscience contribute one penny to their continuance. This is a matter not of law but of expedience. It is not that public forms of gambling are wrong, but that at the moment they ought to be discouraged. In happier times or in another country, conscience may interpose no bar. But here and now, duty towards the weaker brethren demands that we do nothing which can make it easier for them to stumble.

And there can be no question that, if conscientious persons in England boycotted the use of public forms of gambling on these grounds, their example would be infectious; the demand would fall, and the gambling habit be restricted to proper proportions. That conscientious persons should be meticulous not to overstep the bounds of amusement and recreation in their own gambling goes without saying. That they should resolutely frown on and discourage all obvious excess in others is a matter of course. But something further is needed. At the moment they should abstain from all public gambling altogether; they should deny themselves even that moderate amount which is legitimate to them. And, if they derive great amusement from this particular form of recreation, let them confine themselves to betting with their friends, and running sweepstakes in the privacy of their own intimate circles. In the public interest this is surely no great hardship to endure.

To the question, then, 'May I buy a ticket in the Irish sweep, or bet with a bookie on a racecourse?' the answer would be, 'In other circumstances you might, but things being as they are at present, you ought not'.

Note. This essay was already in type before the contents of the Bill dealing with lotteries, &c., recently introduced in the House of Lords, were made public.

VII. ETHICS AND RELIGION

By J. S. BEZZANT

ETHICS and religion result from two deep and interlacing activities of personality. History and experience show that they are connected yet distinguishable, and also that the varying degrees of distinctness do not amount to separation. If separation occurs the consequence is damage both to ethics and to religion. Whitehead's warning against the obsession that religion is necessarily a good thing is not superfluous:[1] the survival of inadequately moralized religion, when well-grounded ethics can recognize it as such, probably does more harm than good. It is doubtful whether there has ever been an entirely non-ethical religion, if religion be judged by its contemporary ethical standards; if there has been, then such a religion and religion that has become moralized are two different things, which may be in part historically continuous but have no actual identity in any sense which is significant. Theories of ethics and religion, and of their relations, must take account of these facts, and not do them violence in the interests of abstract consistency.

The distinctions are real: they have often given rise to actual conflict. The moral activity and experience need not contain elements which are inseparable

---

[1] *Religion in the Making*, p. 17.

from the specifically religious activity and experience. Nor need the consequent ethics. Ethics builds on the foundation that the moral consciousness and its judgements of value carry their own authority. The essence of moral obligation is that my duty is my duty whether I like it or not and that plainly it *ought* to be done. A moral judgement is 'subjective' in the sense that it is within the experience of a living subject, but it is essentially *binding* in character. It is recognized as 'objective' at least in the sense that it ought to be equally binding on any other man in exactly the same circumstances. It is therein distinguished from subjective tastes and feelings such as that certain dishes are nice or nasty: these are not 'objectively' either nice or nasty, but are simply nice to one man and nasty to another. We do not seriously say that other persons *ought* to share our tastes in food and drink. But that is a position which ethics can never adopt in regard to moral judgements without ceasing to be moral. When conscience—or reason exercising itself on moral issues—delivers a judgement, we may not, without being immoral, ask or be guided by whether it is pleasant or convenient to act on that judgement.

Nor is the imperative nature or the content of moral demands conceived as deriving from any externally imposed command or from the sanction of God. To perform any acts simply because they are commanded, apart from a confirming judgement of our own insight that they ought to be done—even though such acts may be those commonly reckoned as good—is not to act morally.[1] Such acts may be right but they are not morally right. Indeed, to accept externally prescribed rules, otherwise than by the confirming judgement of conscience that we ought to accept them because they are seen to be right, is at least amoral or non-ethical, and tends to become immoral and un-ethical. Hence a real autonomy or independence of judgement is essential to a moral person and to moral advance, and ethics must insist upon it.

But the experience of moral obligation—that certain actions are right and ought to be done or that they are wrong and ought not to be done—does not itself imply any immediate or direct theological belief; in itself it contains no explicit reference to any such belief. Man can recognize some things as beautiful and value them; but it is a further question, and not an inseparable element in the experience itself, whether beauty is the work of a divine artist, and it is a question which cannot be answered by confining attention to the experience and value of beauty. In the same way man can recognize the imperative or binding nature of judgements of conscience without implying a divine legislator. The reality of God may be and often is thought necessary if the objectivity of

[1] Except, of course, as a means towards the realization of ends which are judged to be morally right and which cannot otherwise be realized. If external commands are accepted in the faith that the doing of what is commanded will lead to personal insight that it is right in itself, the acceptance is moral, and the law originally imposed externally must either become our own right insight or be rejected.

judgements of conscience is to be logically or reasonably justified; it may be thought that the existence of God alone guarantees that moral judgements are values for any Reality beyond human valuers; but such theological belief itself logically presupposes the previous activity of the moral reason.

Religion is always something more than moral activity and of inferences therefrom. Notoriously difficult to define, it is, as Dr. Webb says, 'always a conscious relation or attempt to get into relation with what, however crudely imagined or conceived, is yet imagined or conceived as somehow containing in itself the mysterious power at the heart of things. It thus always involves at least an implicit view or theory of what, when reflection is sufficiently advanced, is seen to be the world or life as a whole, and at last to be the Ultimate Reality.' Morality, on the other hand, apart from religion 'is not, in the same way as religion, essentially a conscious relation to what is within or below or behind or above (we may use which metaphor we will) the "number of things" of which "the world is full" '.[1] Not only so, but as reflection advances, religion, if it is not to become a compromise dangerous to its own health and advance, is seen to demand dependence upon its Object; and not a dependence which begins only when and where

[1] C. C. J. Webb, *A Century of Anglican Theology*, p. 65. The three chapters on Morality and Religion seem to me, if leave to say so may be taken, to be marked by uncommon breadth and depth of judgement, and I refer readers to them for fuller treatment of some of the themes of this essay.

we may find ourselves unable to stand morally in our own strength or by our own insight, but an utter dependence. Here the distinctness between ethics and religion seems to amount to a contradiction and is sometimes accepted as such.

Again it is a fact of experience and of history that the moral and religious capacities are not equally sensitive in different men nor even blended in equal strength in the same man. That the pure in heart shall see God and that religion is vain deceit or deliberate hypocrisy when it does not issue in a more exalted morality than exists without it—these are judgements which could only be made when religion has been moralized in the most penetrating fashion, or when men recognize that it ought to be. In fact, the religious temperament or capacity for religion does exist quite genuinely side by side with moral insensitiveness in the one person; and a man can be intensely aware of the inexorable demands of the moral law without any awakening of his capacity for religion or any explicit recognition of God. History often shows ethics and religion going their own particular ways, and their strained relations are sometimes more apparent than their interaction. Beliefs and practices have been treated as sacred by religion when contemporary ethics has condemned them as unethical, and when religious persons themselves would have condemned such beliefs and practices if applied in other spheres of thought and action. Religion by its nature attaches sacredness to its own

past history and traditions and is thus always conservative. Even when ethical criticism makes itself felt as something other than impiety, religious
reverence always tends rather to allegorize or 'spiritu-
alize' ethically condemned beliefs than to abandon
them frankly, and to feel a sense of loss in giving up
its past practices when ethics no longer approves
them. Religion is never only concerned with knowing: its relations with its Object have some of the marks
of a personal relation even when the Object itself is
not conceived as personal. Man's relations to an imperative moral law are not the only means of his
approach to God, and it is always dangerously easy
to forget, even when the proposition is intellectually
accepted, that they must condition other ways of approach. It lies near at hand to think that God can be
approached in other less exacting and more indulgent
ways. These have a more popular appeal and encourage the idea of special privileges bestowed upon
the friends of God. The demands of morality are
compromised. Mercy is *contrasted* with the moral
law, or with Divine justice, as in the picture of the
Mother of Mercy with outstretched arm to stay the
wrath of her avenging Son. Compromises of this
kind foster consequent superstitions which in popular
religion come to count for more than the essentials
of ethical religion. Transgression and its consequences are thought to be wiped out by non-moral
transactions or non-moral ceremonies. Thus religion loses its spiritual character and morality is cor-

rupted. The personal relation between the believer and God does not become or ceases to be a morally personal relation but issues in impersonal dealings which ethics can only condemn as immoral.

It is from ethics that the most serious criticisms of a religion can come, though they may be long in making themselves felt by the generality of religious people. From the moment it is realized that God is righteous a doctrine or a practice may be condemned as unethical and as false by the moral conscience. If that happens, a doctrine or practice so condemned cannot be maintained or established on any other grounds except at the cost of outraging the very consciousness whereby we may recognize any doctrine to be of God. The more thoroughly a religion is integrated with morality (as in Christianity) the more certainly does progress in that religion and in its theology depend upon keeping this principle steadily in view, and upon increasing sensitiveness to its implications. At least from the time of Amos's great protest against the largely non-moral religion of his day, the work of the prophets of Israel was deeply concerned with securing the full exercise of a growing moral consciousness within the sphere of religion; and we may claim that in Christianity the integration of morality and religion reaches its highest point, with moral freedom not only secured but inspired. For criticism and revision of the doctrinal and moral content of our religion is carried on in the light shed by its own highest values, a work made easier in one sense if more exacting in another by historical methods of study and by Biblical criticism. And such criticism as comes from without is the work of conscience moulded by an environment largely indebted to Christianity.

The last point is significant for another and deeper aspect of our subject. It must not be thought that the relations of ethics and religion are the simple story of religion's debt to autonomous ethics. It is not a fact that sensitive moral conscience and exalted ethics best maintain themselves in practical or theoretical isolation from religion. Ethical theories which teach that it should be so take too narrow a view of human nature, build upon inadequate data, and often mistake abstractions for actualities.

Conscience is not like a sensitive mechanical gauge which, when faced with moral choices, automatically indicates either right or wrong. That is a view of conscience which has often made men weary of its name. It is not infallible; but it is educable; it grows with its own exercise, but to grow rightly it needs the right environment; and the right environment is an ethic grounded in so much of reality as is within our knowledge or may be within our reasonable belief. Most men, though they feel in varying degrees the imperatives of conscience, must be able to believe that the distinctions between right and wrong correspond to something at the heart of things—to reflect the nature of something beyond themselves; otherwise the imperatives tend to become less urgent, and morality to be treated as though it were merely what others think about human conduct. It is as it comes home to them in and through sincere religion that most men feel the constraint of the moral law most strongly; and it is no less a fact that denial of God tends, in the long run, to undermine conviction that morality is objective and binding, even though it may not at once result in conscious rejection of ethics previously held, or in changes of actual conduct. That is at least true—of most of those who reject religion— to an extent which makes the exceptions notable; and the exceptions are not independent of the religion which exercises indirect influence upon them through their environment. No doubt a kind of morality would still be necessary for individual well-being and to hold the community together even in a world in which no one believed in God, or in abiding values to be actualized through right use of the present world, or in immortality, and in which the voice of prayer and praise was nowhere heard; but there is little reason to think that the finer fruits and graces of morality would flourish and increase or even survive in such a secularized society. Notwithstanding the frequent criticism of religion by ethics (which in the long run is accepted by religion) it cannot be denied that progress in morality no less than in religion has largely consisted in and resulted from bringing them together. This fact is more important than the abstract arguments by which some theorists claim ethics as an independent philosophy and deny that religion can speak the last if any word on moral issues. If inadequately moralized religion can easily become something human life would be as well without, there are grave defects in a non-religious ethics which at last make it impotent to save religion from that fate. Moral aspirations within abstract systems of ethics have not inspired anything like the same intensity of devotion found among those who, believing in a holy and personal God, have sought to be made like unto Him. That the universe is the work and an expression of the nature of a personal God is the belief about it within which the hold of morality on the human mind has attained a maximum intensity and extent. The appeal of a living personal influence is far stronger to personal beings than the appeal of abstract theory, however self-consistent; it is the most potent of all moral motive influences. The reverence and love of God—as the love of a Person whose rule of love is the only ultimate power there is, and who is the source and spring of conscience itself no less than of all goodness—is the one emotional influence, whether of a personal or social kind, which will assuredly always support and intensify the demands of morality. If religion be this, then it is something which must slowly permeate all human activities, and most directly the moral, and can never be sharply marked off from them. When such religion does not have these effects its implications are being overlooked, or else obscured by other elements in it which are really inconsistent with its own highest content. Freely to refuse

the evil and to choose the good, according to the pre-
scriptions of ethics, lacks the depth and earnestness
which is characteristic of the religious attitude towards goodness and sin; the rigorously moralist
temper, apart from the atmosphere of living religion,
does not normally or easily exhibit the finer graces of
sympathy and humility which have flourished where
grace is accounted higher than law; and there is much
in the modern world which goes to confirm belief
that, when religious faith decays and theology is considered superfluous, the inexorable demands which
ethics, after separation from religion, may certainly
for a time continue to make, are not in fact maintained. These results may reasonably be thought to
correspond with the nature of man, which is not only
moral, and of the world in which he is set. To say that
they will be otherwise when human evolution is
further advanced is but to make drafts upon the
future which there is little indication and no guarantee that it will honour.

Religion is concerned not only with what ought to
be but also with *what is*. If 'what is' includes God,
moral conduct cannot exclude conduct towards God.
An ethic concerned exclusively with man's relations
with man neither has nor can have any grounds of
confidence that its ideals will ever be actualized, or
that they are anything more than human values. So
far as the content of ethics alone can inform us, the
universe may destroy both us and all our values. The
moral man will reply that even so they ought not to

be regarded as less binding. The religious man entirely agrees, though he may entertain a well-grounded doubt as to whether in fact it will be so. The point is that there may be features about the universe which do not confirm the view of its nature which the moral life of man may seem to indicate. Hence it is only by reference to a wider field than that of purely ethical phenomena that either religion or philosophy can find adequate *grounds* (as distinct from *causes*) of confidence that ethical and other values are more than values *for us*, and that they are 'intimations of that Ultimate Reality whose essential attributes are manifested therein'.

Ethics alone cannot decide ultimate questions about the nature of the universe and of man; while the answers to those questions will in practice have profound effects upon human conduct and ethical theories. Some uphold materialistic naturalism as the sufficient account of existence. Man is then a part of a mindless and purposeless Nature: the real stuff of man is the impulses, cravings, and passions which he shares with the animals of whom he is but the cleverest. Ideals, including moral ideals, in the last resort are dream-work. Many practical and emotional considerations may then maintain as a conventional standard the morality which has been built up on other views of man; but it is not likely either that the Naturalist will be uninfluenced by his doctrine of the world and of man, or that his conscience will deliver the same judgements, or judgements of the same urgency, as the conscience of the Humanist for whom man, his civilization and culture are the highest realities the universe contains. Again, the Humanist may regard the service of humanity and of human culture as the all-sufficient inspiration of human conduct; he may treat religious beliefs and inspiration as flimsy imaginings no longer needed by human nature which has grown to full stature; and he may profess indifference to the issue whether human cultural values bear any relation to realities of abiding and eternal worth. If so it is unlikely that either his moral judgement or his ethical theory will be the same as those of the ethical Theist or the Christian who believes that man bears the image of God to whom nothing that is not good may be ascribed, and whose rule is the only final power; that the universe admits of fellowship with God; and that the meaning of human life is not exhausted in the visible and material world, nor confined within the limits of the present life therein. But in deciding between the claims of materialistic Naturalism, Humanism, and Christianity to be true, other considerations besides those of purely ethical phenomena must be taken into account; though, if there are other grounds of reasonable faith that the universe is teleological, the ethical life of man will appear the most important factor as indicating what at least part of the purposed end is. Man's moral conscience will then tell him most about the purpose and character of God, and other elements in his relationship to God will be subordinated to and conditioned by the moral relationship.

The conception of the nature of ethics which best accords alike with the history of ethics and of human moral life, and which is also most congenial to religion, is that ethics is neither 'a science of absolute values' nor a matter of merely individual and subjective likes and dislikes. Ethical judgements do indeed claim to be right, true, and imperative, independently of the agreement of particular individuals; they are right in all normal circumstances and may be 'practically absolute'. But it does not follow that they are right unconditionally or universally: that is an unnecessary and unjustified theoretical leap. In fact we cannot lay down the simplest ethical maxim as being right in itself regardless of all circumstances, consequences, or stages of human development.[1] Such maxims will be found to have no significance apart from specific persons and circumstances; and their application by those persons in those circumstances is always something of a venture, never a merely cautious and sensible adjustment of action to *a priori* certainties. It is in making the venture conscientiously

___

[1] On this point (as on much else relevant to the relations of ethics and religion) see *The Threshold of Ethics*, by K. E. Kirk, pp. 29 ff. It is because certain sets of circumstances prevail very widely and remain practically constant that we can apply certain ethical maxims by 'rule of thumb' methods, without the sense of venture. But there is no guarantee that the circumstances will always prevail or prevail universally; a situation may at any time arise in which a judgement of conscience is required to decide whether any such maxim as 'Always do so-and-so' or 'Never do so-and-so' does or does not apply.

that moral conduct consists, that ethical insight is deepened, and moral progress advanced.

'From the desired to the desirable, from the concrete good, that is good for something, to the good in itself, from the sub-personal to the over-individual, and from the social to what may be called the over-social or the absolute, there is a way. But there is no deductive way back from high abstractions, so reached, to particular moral judgements relevant to specific Actual issues. Necessary truth, in ethics as anywhere else, is purchased at the price of possible irrelevance to Actuality, and therefore—in one sense —of meaninglessness. . . . It may prove to be concerned with abstract concepts to which names can be given, but which have no denotation.'[1]

History and experience show that it is in the setting of living religion that morality maintains its securest hold and the teachings of ethics attain maximum influence. It is obvious that the generally accepted level of morality has been far below the standards of the religiously inspired ethics of Jesus. But it is equally clear that religion can only be kept spiritual, sane, and free of superstition, so long as it is fully integrated with and permeated by the highest attainments of ethical insight. Religion has, in fact, often sanctioned

[1] F. R. Tennant, *Philosophical Theology*, vol. i, p. 153 f. The chapter on 'Valuation and Theory of Ethical Value' is a drastic criticism of 'absolutist' ethics. It is such ethical theory, and ethics as a kind of phenomenology dealing with essences said to be apprehended by an intuition at once immediate and self-evident, by which the most irreconcilable antinomies between ethics and religion may easily be set up.

doctrines and practices condemned by the more enlightened and sensitive moral consciences, and has
claimed to override their judgements in moral issues.
The ethical demand for moral independence is as
thoroughgoing as the religious demand for dependence upon God. Yet a religion which limits the freedom of morality thereby degrades it; while a moral
legalism in alliance with religion will always appear as
a formalizing if not as a corruption of true religion.
Hence, in spite of the warnings of history and the facts
of experience, there is a modern tendency in ethical
theory to detach morals from the inspiration, motives,
and authority of religion, while allowing religion to
be autonomous in its own sphere. Boundary lines
are drawn; fundamental contradictions are unrecon-
ciled; isolated religion looks askance at the appeal to
conscience as rebellion against God, while ethics must
needs regard communion with God and dependence
on Divine grace as inconsistent with true morality
and as weakening moral personality.

An outstanding instance of this position will be
found in the great treatise on ethics by Hartmann.[1]
In this work it is fully recognized that there is a deep
inward connexion between ethics and religion; but
there is a boundary line between their respective
domains. Critical ethical philosophy has 'set up barriers against the dictatorial aggression of religious

---

[1] *Ethics*, by Nicolai Hartmann, particularly vol. iii, ch. xx.
(Authorized translation by Stanton Coit in The Library of
Philosophy.)

thought'; it has become 'independent master' of certain ethical problems with which religion has dealt and still deals; and thereby 'at the same time secures the independence of religion within its own boundaries'. In religion ethical problems come under a point of view different from that essential to ethics. This in itself is no occasion for conflict. It may be, Hartmann says, that religion constitutes a higher stratum in which the contents of ethics 'show themselves in a new and more significant aspect'; and continues:

'That in Idea such a relationship may hold good, we may quietly assume without doing violence to one or the other domain, so long at least as we keep in mind that it is only an assumption. Moreover, the circumstances are by no means such that the emergence of contradictions destroys the value of such an assumption. Antinomies prove nothing against the co-existence of what is antinomically divided, even though they should prove to be genuine antinomies, that is, should be insoluble. They only prove the inability of thought to comprehend the co-existence.'

This learned writer is fully aware that there are many facts which seem to justify both sides of the alleged antinomies between ethics and religion. But 'whoever takes his stand on one of them, to him the opposite side will always seem unnatural, violent, preposterous. But precisely such preposterousness is characteristic of the whole problem.' His final word is that it is not ethics but the philosophy of religion which conjures up these antinomies.

Fundamental in Hartmann's ethical philosophy is a

kind of apriorism and absolutism which cannot be
examined here. The alleged contradictions between
the demands of ethics and of religion may be sharp-
ened by that philosophy, but they have often been
urged on the basis of like ethical philosophies. Ethics
expounded and maintained as 'a science of absolute
values' is inconsistent with knowledge about how we
come to know and with how in fact we have attained
the ethical values we recognize. If we may take ethical
experience as absolute it is not clear why we may not
take scientific experience of the physical world as
absolute; which if we do we must needs adhere to a
materialistic naturalism which leaves no grounds for
any view of ethics as dealing with more than subjective preferences, which then do not allow us to infer
anything from them about the nature of reality.

Ethical experience is but part, if a profound part,
of human experience. A philosophy built exclusively
upon it can no more claim to be absolute than can a
philosophy built exclusively upon the data of natural
science, or a theology built only upon the distinctive
elements in religious experience, and ignoring the
implications of other experience and knowledge of
the world. Absolutist ethics on the one hand, and on
the other a conception of religion and theology which
assumes that we are able to prescribe what it befits
omnipotence and omniscience to do, and then to argue
downwards from God, will always lead to insoluble
antinomies between ethics and religion. The antinomies are less insoluble if, alike in ethics and theo-

logy, we reason from our actual experience and from the way in which God actually deals with sons who bear His image.

The fundamental consideration which preserves inviolate the moral freedom essential to ethics, and which alone keeps religious dependence spiritual, is that the religious relationship with God is not *any* kind of relationship, such as one in which man is dominated by a God who is impersonal force, but that it is a *personal* relationship.[1] This is the key to the solution of many otherwise insoluble antinomies, some of which we will briefly consider.

It is frequently contended that for ethics nothing, neither God nor any fiat of His power, stands behind moral values and our duties in regard to them; and it is represented that for religion it is only because moral claims are regarded as Divine commands that their contents are felt to be moral values.

Now no doubt some religious teaching gives ground for drawing such a contrast, but nothing consistent with a truly moralized religion does so. On the contrary, the fact is that where there is full consciousness of personality, reflection upon the sacredness of judgements of conscience has itself often seemed to point to, if not to require, a personal Law-giver.

[1] It is the thorough-going application of this principle, in an outlook which neither evades the implications of modern knowledge bearing on religion nor tones down the requirements of religion, which makes Dr. John Oman's little book *Grace and Personality* such a valuable contribution to modern theology. My debt to it is very great.

A personal relation to Him is then felt to be a more truly moral relation than is obedience to an impersonal and abstract moral law. The moral law is not then thought of as something externally prescribed by God, because the idea of God then includes the idea that God himself works with man, never otherwise than through man's reason and willing nor ever by over-bearing them. God as personal Spirit transcends the moral consciousness of man made in His image, but His will cannot, in a personal relationship, be known except as it is one with the manifest authority implicit in man's moral consciousness and experience.

This has the closest bearing upon the further alleged contradiction that ethics is concerned only with man while religion is concerned wholly with God, so that God is everything and man nothing. It is said to be an ethical perversion that even God should take precedence of man, whereas religion regards man's will as good or bad according as it recognizes God's will, and either does or does not humbly set it above his own.

Here again much religious language could be quoted which would support such assertions. But in fact no truly religious and moral person who conceives of his relation to God as a personal relation (which God always respects, or why has he made us persons and not just things?) feels any contradiction between reliance upon his own conscience and his dependence upon God; he neither measures his own will against God's, nor feels his duty towards God and his duty towards man to be alien to each other. In the last resort the religious man excludes nothing from the judgement of the moral conscience. It is only because he can recognize goodness in its own light that he has any sure means of knowing what the will of God is : were it not so, he would be without a standard by which to judge of doctrines whether they be of God. It is always an important duty to see that the moral reason is enlightened and sensitive; moreover both religion and morality are thoroughly social, and we may not rightly judge as mere individualists without proper regard to the judgements of our brethren in society and in the church. But in the last resort the religious man no less than the moralist cannot hold anything to be right or wrong, good or bad, if conscience persistently decrees to the contrary. There can be no ultimate conflict between the moral will of the religious man and the will of God if that be also a moral will. Thus the Christian accepts the teaching of Christ as authoritative : it is authoritative in character in the sense that it is all 'verily, verily', and is not tentatively deduced from doubtful premisses. But neither on that account nor on any other does Jesus ever suggest that his teaching is absolved from commending itself before the tribunal of conscience. On the contrary, its authority and its strength lie precisely in its power of self-authentication before that tribunal—in the 'Amen' which it calls forth from the moral conscience. It is not otherwise with St. Paul; he teaches with authority, but he expressly writes of 'commending ourselves to every man's conscience in the sight of God'. It is in the individual mind and conscience that religion no less than ethics must establish its strength and its certainties if it is ever to have any effective measure of either among thoughtful men. If religion is a personal relation to God, even the Divine gift of faith cannot be given and is not spiritual except as it can increasingly become our own insight freely recognized and acted upon. The truth is well put by Dr. Oman: 'To be independent moral persons, legislating for ourselves, so far from being hostile to true knowledge and right service of God, is the imperative condition without which God can neither be known nor served.'[1]

The personal response of the human conscience and will which God requires, and which alone is a personal relation at all, can only be given as we see and accept the will of God to be good. It is the independence of the moral conscience which increasingly determines our whole relation to God; without it there can be no personal dependence upon God, for God's will and the moral order are one and cannot be imposed by any other reason than the reason why we judge it to be right. Only so can we know it to be a Divine decree. 'Only by being true to ourselves can we find the reality which we must absolutely follow, yet only by the sense of a reality which we must absolutely follow can we be true to ourselves.' It is not strange that history and experience, which show the

[1] *Grace and Personality*, p. 53.

practical consequences which follow from sincerely
held beliefs, also testify to the damage which ensues
both to morality and to religion from separating
either from the other; and ethics and theology dare
not effect the separation in the interests of a formal
and abstract theoretical consistency, and at the cost
of violence to what is actual.

It may further be urged that it is only in abstract
ethical theory such as is aloof from fact that morality,
without religion, can maintain its own essential independence. Man's recognition of the demands of the
moral law is one thing; his ability to fulfil them is
another; the consequences of his inability are yet another. The most exacting of moral demands is that we
should seek to judge with an ever increasing and more
penetrating conscientiousness.[1] But has man the
power to actualize every ideal of which he can conceive? Is it enough to prescribe 'You can because you
ought'? The answer of experience is not in doubt. Experience shows that the prescription is likely to be re-
versed so as to read 'You ought not when you cannot'.
This results in contentment with easy-going standards,
in conventionality, and in the ossification and deteri-
oration of morals. And even in theory it is not reasonable to think of human moral capacity as though the
actual conditions of human nature, the character of
the world, its meaning and purpose, and the kind or
degree of independence it allows, were all of no consequence. We are certainly not independent in the

[1] See K. E. Kirk, *The Threshold of Ethics*, pp. 144 ff.

sense that we can ignore reality without disaster, whether in morals or in anything else. Once again we have the position that ethical questions cannot be cut off from the questions 'What are we?' and 'In what kind of world do we live?' And ethics alone cannot answer those questions. Only if man may depend on a reality and a will greater than his own, which work with him and are reflected in his own conscience, will he be inspired and able to judge with an ever increasing and more penetrating conscientiousness.

So long as a man thinks and tries to act as though his whole moral position is that he stands in isolated independence face to face with the demands of an abstract moral law, one of two results will occur, and neither is in the long run anything but fatal to deep and progressive moral character. If such a man's conception of the moral law's demands is moderate or low, or if his self-criticism in the light of the moral law (high or low) is superficial, his moral condition will take rank accordingly, and he will become more or less self-satisfied. 'All these things have I kept.' He will not easily be moved to add 'What lack I yet?', and he will certainly not go on doing so indefinitely. If his conception of the moral law's demands is penetrating and his self-criticism rigorous he will feel keenly his inability to rise to what is demanded; when in addition he realizes that his inability so to rise has been increased by his own past failures, he will find himself menaced by defeat leading to despair, unless in self-defence he falls back to a moral level in which the contents of 'I ought' are determined by what 'I can'. So far from maintaining his moral independence and increasing it, he will become dependent on conventional standards. Both self-satisfaction and despair are self-centred. Not only do they rob moral life of that disinterestedness which is its finest grace and virtue,[1] but they sap the very independence which is morally essential. It is only the independence which is born of dependence on a reality greater than self, which also ever calls and leads us on, which is the real life-principle of growth in man's moral consciousness. Such dependence is not unethical because the reality itself is not alien to, though it transcends, the moral conscience, and because it cannot be followed except by our own insight. The reason for dependence is the reason why we ought to be dependent, and in fact are so. The assistance of the grace of God, when religion is a personal relation to God, is no more immoral, though it is infinitely more all-embracing and effectual, than are the support and encouragement in moral life which come through human personal and social relationships. For God's grace is not something which moves and inclines our wills except through our willing consent. This dependence on the will and grace of God is in fact a relation

[1] See further, and especially on the point that the life of worship alone guarantees humility and self-forgetfulness, K. E. Kirk's Bampton Lectures on *The Vision of God*, ch. viii; the same author's *The Threshold of Ethics*, ch. vi; and his Broadcast lecture in *God and the World through Christian Eyes*, second series.

which confers the needed freedom to do as we ought
to do: it is a personal relation inclusive of God and
man, never something arbitrarily imposed by God's
superior might or achieved by our *blind* submission.
Thus it is that any separation of moral independence
from religious dependence, as Dr. Oman says, divides
a living reality in the interests of abstract explana-
tions: the personal relation which religion is, and
which is the unfailing succour of moral persons, then
disappears.

It is sometimes contended that the doctrine of
Divine Providence is irreconcilable with the free
scope of human wills which ethics requires. If God's
rule is the determining factor and is an almighty
power, over against it man is impotent. This is a
matter which concerns not only the relations of ethics
and religion: it concerns religion itself. For if religion is a personal relation to God, that relation can
never be effected by the sheer unqualified power of
God; whereas if it may only be effected by the constraining power of love, that is no more at variance
with human freedom than is the constraining power
of the imperatives of moral demands. It is as indispensable to true freedom as true freedom is to it.
Religion is not concerned to set up a conception of
Divine Providence inconsistent with the personality
which the same Providence has conferred upon His
children. If God's rule is the only ultimate constraining power, it does not, if it be a rule of love, actualize
itself among men except as they freely recognize and

accept it. It is not as an answer to a purely theoretical problem that it is affirmed that God shall be all in all: it is the affirmation of faith. To admit, in the realm of abstract theory, that God's rule may never be universally actualized does not inhibit the faith that it will be, and without which it cannot be if it is to remain a rule of love.

Another alleged contradiction between ethics and religion is that whereas ethics, even in its most far-reaching ideals, confines attention to this world, religion looks to a Beyond. Religion, it is said, thus tends to depreciate the present world and present experience in a way which inevitably discourages whole-hearted dealing with them, even if it does not set up the ideal of a complete escape from the world. Moral striving, on the contrary, regards concern with anything which transcends this life as the chasing of a deceitful phantom.

The religious man will reply that morality does not exhaust the whole life of the human spirit, and that the purely ethical interpretation of the world, though true, is not the complete truth. If man and the fashion of this world pass away, man must look to a Beyond if his moral values are not in the end to be fruitless. The sincerely moral and religious man does not look to a Beyond with a yearning inspired by any desire to escape from the present world and its duties: he does so because the present is not otherwise to be estimated aright. What is of eternal and abiding worth to the soul is not to be won except by the sincere and thorough use of and dealing with the present world of actual duties and opportunities, even though these are transient. The most far-seeing ethical ideals are not realized here, and to trim them to what is so realizable would be as disastrous to ethics as false to religious faith. It is precisely the contrast between the ethical 'ought to be' and the present 'is' which requires the Beyond if deep ethical insight is not impracticable and misleading dreaming; though religion may be already conscious of the reality of the Beyond in other ways and, partly at least, on other grounds.

We may conclude by considering briefly a contradiction alleged to exist between the requirements of ethics and what has always been fundamental in and distinctive of Christianity—its doctrine of forgiveness. This is held to be unethical because sin cannot be done away. Man must bear its weight or be weighed down by it: ethics cannot go beyond that position; and in any case, it is said, 'there is, in principle, no incapacity in man to be good due to his guilt'. To take away guilt is to violate freedom and therefore to violate personality, and is a greater evil than the bearing of guilt. Religion, it is said, regards sin not as guilt before the court of conscience and of ethical values, but as guilt before God. Hartmann goes so far as to say that an extreme form of the religious view could be popularly expressed thus: 'Never mind what you do, let happen what will, if only you do not have to bear the guilt, for before God guilt is the offence.'

Now whatever else is doubtful, it is certain that for

ethical religion nothing would more imperatively
demand penitence, without which forgiveness is impossible, than the attitude described in the words just
quoted. It is equally certain that responsibility for
our actions remains. That fact is perhaps the most
certain ground of our continuous self-consciousness.
Nor is any feature of the religious consciousness more
striking than its imputation of wrong-doing to the
self, though all its goodness may be ascribed to the
grace of God. Further, for religion no less than for
ethics, human life is largely what it is because the consequences of moral wrong-doing are what they are.
Forgiveness is not directed to the cancelling of those
consequences otherwise than by overcoming the
wrongs of which they are the consequences. It is
rather a Divine grace which enables man to accept
the consequences in a new spirit, and thereby to rise
above both the consequences and the sins. Unforgiven sin may have consequences which forgiveness
will prevent, partly because the consequences of continuing in an unforgiven state are cumulative, and
partly because, in the state of forgiveness, the very
results of sin may become further occasions of goodness and of grace: in dealing with them aright, which
forgiveness enables us to do, and in helping the infir-
mities of others which may be partly the result of sin,
good can be and is brought out of evil. It is only while
man is yet untouched by forgiveness that he is concerned with evading the consequences of sin; and it
is from such evasion and the further paralysing effects

thereof that it is the purpose of forgiveness to set him free. Forgiveness is no longer an outrage of the demand of the moral law that the punishing consequences of its violation must be borne, when forgiveness is such that 'the acceptance of it by the person forgiven does the office of punishment'. It is, as Dr. Webb says, not by the intention of the forgiver but through the awakened conscience of the person forgiven that coals of fire are heaped upon his head.

When it is said that 'there is, in principle, no incapacity to be good' due to man's guilt, 'in principle' can only mean 'in theory'. In experience there is no doubt that it is otherwise unless, indeed, the conception of guilt is superficial. Even to realize with sufficiently penetrating insight what in the present is morally demanded of us is to realize that we cannot fulfil the moral law's demands. And if, as cannot be doubted, we are even less able to fulfil them by reason of the cumulative effects of our past failures than we might otherwise have been, we are not only unprofitable servants now, and must for ever so remain: we must inevitably become more so. There is then not only no assurance of victory, but an actual menace of defeat which either hampers our efforts to a degree which results in an unethical self-centredness fatal to the attainment of the higher moral graces, or else drives us to seek relief and peace in moral insensitiveness and insincerity. Herein is our deep need. Forgiveness deals with it, not by a superficial condoning of our condition, or by any pretence that it is other than it

is, but by really making it something else. It does
not work either impersonally or unethically. It does
not enable us to overcome evil as easily as we yield
to it, but it confers an insight into our true place in
God's world and in His family, and so transforms
our world into one in which, in fellowship with God,
all things are possible which are consistent with
righteousness and love. If the result is to free us from
the domination of certain sins 'which live only in the
dark' ti is by conscious insight into God's gracious
goodness and not by any kind of unethical or sub-
personal change in the self. Thus the ends of ethics
are attained or rendered attainable as they can never
be so long as our true condition is held to be simply
a legal relation to an impersonal law or to impersonal
values. Ethics, so conceived, is an abstraction from
the reality of our position in the world and cannot
confer the power by which alone its own demands
can be fulfilled. This comes only with our restoration
to our true relation to God as a personal Spirit and to
our true place in the world and family of God 'whom
to serve is to reign'.